D0668898

Also by Peter James Flamming

Healing the Heartbreak of Grief

Poking Holes in the Darkness, & 14 Other
Sermons You Just Can't Sleep Through

God and Creation

Never Stop Starting

ONE DOZEN LESSONS FOR A VIBRANT LATER LIFE

God bless you!

Peter James Flamming

Peter James Flamming

WESTBOW
PRESS®
A DIVISION OF THOMAS NELSON
& ZONDERVAN

Cover Photo by Shirley Flamming; Author Photo by Ann Cook

WestBow Press books may be ordered through booksellers or by contacting:

WestBow Press
A Division of Thomas Nelson & Zondervan
1663 Liberty Drive
Bloomington, IN 47403
www.westbowpress.com
1 (866) 928-1240

ISBN: 978-1-5127-3594-9 (sc)
ISBN: 978-1-5127-3596-3 (hc)
ISBN: 978-1-5127-3595-6 (e)

Library of Congress Control Number: 2016905242

Print information available on the last page.

WestBow Press rev. date: 05/11/2016

To my wife Shirley
who more than any other person I know
has lived a full life
and Never Stopped Starting!

Contents

Acknowledgments

This book came about because Ray Inscoe invited me to speak on the challenges of later life. As the director of Pastoral Care at Westminster-Canterbury, a retirement community in Richmond, Virginia, Ray hoped I would present a series of lectures for his residents—as part of their "Seminary Mondays" program. I was a bit reluctant. After more than half a century of full-time ministry, I had retired, and the Lord had put three purposes on my horizon—to write, to teach, and to pray. Giving a series of lectures on later life was not what I was expecting to do.

Eventually I felt led to say yes to Ray, and I am very glad I did. I am forever grateful for his invitation, which forced me to think in new ways about familiar topics and to dig deeply into research on aging—a task that altered my views on the stages of our lives and opened my eyes to the many useful ways the Bible speaks to the challenges and opportunities of later life. The first set of lectures was so favorably received that a second round was called for. That too came to pass. And from those sets of lectures came this book, which turned out to be the book I needed to be writing anyway.

To the residents of Westminster-Canterbury, Richmond, I have this to say: You are wonderful! Thank you for welcoming me into your community and for your keen interest in my lectures. What's more, your thoughtful questions and insightful observations enriched my perspective on aging and encouraged me to write this book. It is certainly a much better book because of your contributions.

Having a book in mind is one thing; bringing it to fruition is another. My eternal thanks for the lives and work of Theresa Norton and Deborah Hocutt, who, quite literally, made the writing and publication of this book possible. From the beginning, Theresa believed in me and in this book. More than anyone, she remained insistent that I stick with my *writing*, even when I would have rather been thinking about what I *might* write. Deborah helped me turn a cluster of loosely crafted lectures into a coherent book; her fruitful recommendations have been beyond number. Thank you, Theresa and Deborah!

My family helped, too, in so many ways. My son, Douglas, and my granddaughter, Elizabeth, read and edited the manuscript as it moved through various stages. My son, J. Dee, enthusiastically financed the editing process offered by WestBow Press. My wife, Shirley, and my sister-in-law, Ann Cook, offered useful suggestions for the book and an abundance of love and encouragement for its author.

The First Baptist Church of Richmond, Virginia, where I was pastor for many years, generously provided funds for the publication of this book. FBC Richmond remains my spiritual home, and the church family has continued to shower my family and me with love. I cannot find words enough to express my gratitude for, and love of, the church, which continues to embrace me and to teach me through my later life.

During the final stages of preparing this book, FBC Richmond held a celebration to honor my sixtieth year as an ordained minister. (Talk about later life!) That celebration brought to mind the congregations that had called me to be their pastor over those six decades—from my first church in Eastland, Texas, to Royal Lane Baptist in Dallas, and on through many years at First Baptist Church, Abilene, Texas. Then on to Richmond. Each congregation blessed my life in many special ways, and each helped in shaping the views I put forth in this book. To one and all, may the Lord bless you and keep you.

Looking back, I recall with special fondness a few members who were vital to my spiritual and ministerial growth. Often journeying through their own later life, they became mentors and advisors for the youthful minister I used to be. They are too many to mention here, and most have gone to be with the Lord. But I want to salute them in gratitude and trust that they will know. Rich in spirit and wisdom, their timely counsel helped me more than they could possibly have known. Their lives continue to bless mine.

Last month brought another happy anniversary in my life. My wife and I celebrated our sixtieth year of marriage! Forever young, creative, and vibrant, Shirley has been the light of my life through the many stages of our lives together. To say she has been the foremost blessing in my life does not even scratch the surface. An artist in her own right, she designed the beautiful and inspiring cover for this book, which I dedicate to her with deep and abiding love.

Introduction

A few years ago, my wife and I went to see some new work by Frances Buckalew, a Richmond artist known for her excellent watercolors and equally exquisite murals. Throughout her life, Frances had been many things: a wife, a mother, a grandmother, a great-great grandmother, a teacher, and, of course, an artist. On the day Shirley and I went to see her latest project, she was up on a ladder painting a mural for an assisted living community. In fact, Frances Buckalew was a *resident* of that community. The artist on the ladder that day, the one bringing her vision to life with skill and verve, was 97 at the time.

Part of me felt a sense of amazement that someone who was nearing the century mark could still ply her craft so well. Another part of me recognized Frances Buckalew as part of larger trend in longevity and purposeful living in every stage of our lives.

I was born into the Great Depression—and the Dust Bowl at that. Immediate survival, not longevity, was my family's concern. In those days, life expectancy wasn't what it is now, and the word "old" carried negative connotations. Even policy makers sympathetic to the plight of the nation's senior citizens often spoke of "the elderly" as a "social problem" that needed solving. That deep-seated part of me felt particularly amazed at Frances Buckalew's work that day.

I was also a minister for more than fifty years, beginning in the 1950s, and that calling provided me with the opportunity to witness changing trends in my own congregations. Slowly but surely, I became aware that the senior members of my church were living longer. What's more, they were remaining more active in all aspects of life, inside and outside of the church. That part of me saw Frances Buckalew's work as part of a new normal.

Better nutrition, better medical possibilities, and better exercise patterns have led to some amazing changes. The fastest growing segment of the American population is people above the age of 85. And if we look further we find that the number of centenarians, those reaching 100 (and then some!) is on the uptick. Almost all of us know someone who has passed the century mark. These days, the question is not whether we will live longer than our parents. I have, and a significant number of us will.

Our new longevity raises a very important question: What are we going to do with the final years of our lives? I wrote this book to help you answer that question. *Never Stop Starting* offers basic principles for living a vibrant and meaningful later life.

The first step is recognizing that the choice is yours to make. A man in his eighties said to me some years ago, "I dread getting older than I already am. All I have to look forward to is to die." That kind of thinking is what we need to avoid. It is best to jettison the attitudes we have toward growing old altogether, because they are deeply rooted, cultivated from negative connotations in our culture. Instead, accept that the final years of life are a new stage of development, a stage that will have its full share of both challenges and opportunities. Let's reframe the way we think about later life.

As a minister, part of my calling was to be there for people along their life's journey, including at the end of life. So, this book will also reflect the reality that far too many people were lost before they reached later life. If you've walked that path of darkness and grief, the trends and statistics on longevity are cold comfort. I know that pain, losing my own son, Dave Flamming, to leukemia when he was only 33 years old. It would be my prayer that you, like me, have been able to work through the heartbreak. Eventually I was able to write a book for those who were also struggling with grief.[1] With the Lord's help, I learned that those of us who remain are nonetheless called to live meaningful lives and to make the world around us a little better for as long as we can. I offer a chapter in this book on grief, for it will invariably be a heavy part of our final stage of life.

We have good reason to think of our lives as unfolding in stages. For the past century, influential scholars have been studying the stages of human life. In the late 1970s, the psychologist Daniel Levinson published *The Seasons of a Man's Life* and the literary journalist Gail Sheehan published *Passages*. Both books were best sellers, and they made the idea of life-stages a widely accepted part of our national mindset. (Both authors, by the way, have continued to write productively into their later lives, with Levinson recently publishing *The Seasons of a Woman's Life* and Sheehan offering us *New Passages*.) In more recent decades, scholars from many disciplines and writers from many different vantage points have continued to explore the stages of human life.[2]

Although there is disagreement about the details of when each stage begins (and even how many stages there are), let's not get hung up on those issues. Let's focus instead on how we might rethink the stages of our lives and fill each with purpose and meaning. The sociologists Robert S. Weiss and Scott A. Bass have compiled an important collection of essays entitled *Challenges of the Third Age*.[3] Third Age has become a widely used phrase for later life. Just to be clear at the outset, I will use the phrases "third stage" and "final third" as synonyms for "later life."

If we accept a broad and flexible definition of later life, we can focus less on the timing of it and more on how we might discover exciting possibilities. The chapters that follow are not intended to reach only those readers within a narrow age range. Instead, they offer fundamental lessons about life that will be applicable to a wide range of people, from middle-aged bankers to centenarian painters, from those living in longtime family homes to those living in retirement communities, from those who are cared for *and* for their caregivers.

Never Stop Starting, then, is my contribution to the growing literature on later life. Given my long years as a pastor, it shouldn't surprise anyone that my approach is grounded in a spiritual point of view. But having immersed myself in the scholarly literature, what fascinates me most is that academic scholarship and religious views of the aging process have been steadily converging. Almost all writers on the subject agree that *spiritual dimensions play a key role in leading a healthier, more productive later life.*

With the Franciscan monk and writer Richard Rohr, I believe that there is a certain "brightness" that we discover in later life.[4] As for me, my body has seen its best days, but my spiritual self seems as alive as ever, and I am finding new and unexpected ways to be productive.

Each chapter within focuses on a character (or duo) in a Bible story. Each character's story offers a lesson—a discovery—we can apply to our own later lives. Some of these biblical figures will be well known: Moses, for example, and Mary, the Mother of Jesus. Others might be less familiar, such as Barnabas, Esther, and Naomi.

Even if you know the Bible very well, I encourage you to view these biblical characters as if you were encountering their stories for the very first time. I have been reading Bible stories since I could read, and I have preached sermons on all of the characters featured in this book. But until recently, I had never really viewed their stories *through the prism of later life*. When I did so, I was amazed and delighted by all of the lessons on later life found within the Old and New Testaments. It was thrilling to read the Bible again for the very first time, so to speak, and I hope some of the thrill of discovery rubs off on you as you make your way through the book.

Even if you know nothing at all about the Bible, you are most welcome. Bible stories are interesting and easy to follow, and they have a universality that allows them to speak to everyone. These biblically based lessons are intended for anyone and everyone, believers and non-believers alike.

The essential message here is found in the title: *Never Stop Starting*. In every stage of life, we have much to learn. In every stage of life, we begin again. The phrase "never stop starting" reflects a foundational principle of life. It reflects the way God operates in the world and in our individual lives. It is a universal dynamic that applies to all of us. It is God's way. And it is a way filled with hope.

Never Stop Starting offers an essential lesson for living the final third of our lives, and here is what it tells us: *In God's grace, every ending is also a new beginning.*

CHAPTER 1

The Moses Discovery:
Repacking Your Bags on Purpose

*Finally, be strong in the Lord and
in the strength of his power.*
—Ephesians 6:10

The Moses Discovery

Repacking Your Bags on Purpose

Sociologists and gerontologists divide our lives into three segments or ages. The first age is our formative years of childhood, growth, education, and preparation for a vocation. The second age describes the middle years of life. Maybe we leave home, graduate from a college or university, find work, marry, have children, and so on. During these years, vocation largely defines our purposes in life. Many describe these years as the prime of life. Eventually, these years come to an end and we enter the third segment or third age of life. The third age is often considered retirement and beyond. What has been is no more. What will be is often obscured and even frightening.

Sara Lawrence-Lightfoot, author of *The Third Chapter*, interviewed those who had recently retired and were moving into what she calls the third chapter of life. One participant said of the experience, "Suddenly I was in the wilderness with very little in the way of a fundamental core of selfhood." Another, who had been an organizational consultant for large institutions, agencies, foundations, universities, and non-profits, spoke of a "lethargy and a listlessness" after her retirement. She described it as a "chasm of emptiness."[1]

Part of the reason for her emptiness is that if we look outward, we often find our culture places little value on this later stage of life. We are accustomed to receiving affirmation and even commendation during the second age of life. But in the third age, we may feel that there is mostly silence.

Successful author and career counselor Richard J. Leider has much to tell us in *The Power of Purpose*. His ideas about repacking our bags on purpose have helped inform my views of the Moses discovery. In another book, Leider related a personal experience that has important implications for those of us facing later life. During his twentieth walking safari in Tanzania, he and his companions came upon the Hazda tribe. The safari group was honored that night by a huge bonfire and were invited to sit nearest the fire with the tribe's elders. In that culture, the elders of the tribe sit closest to the fire; behind them are the younger adults, and the youth and children are in the back. Leider couldn't help contrasting it to American culture, where the youth get the attention and the oldest are lost in the shadows, often unnoticed and forgotten.[2]

3

We have to face this cultural norm. In the third age, meaning and purpose are *not* going to come from outside sources. Our parents and other key influences are no longer there to guide and affirm us. In fact, if they've lived long enough, we may be the ones affirming them. Our vocation or work, which earlier gave us a place and affirmed our worth, is no longer there. We may be remembered on special days, but on all of the other days, our affirmation and value has to come from within.

In the first two stages of life, affirmation and direction often come from others or from our occupation. That's why upon retirement, most of us feel lost. But eventually

> *We can shrivel up and wait for the end of life, or we can move through the transition toward a new beginning.*

we must realize that what has been cannot be repeated. If we can listen with the spiritual ears of our hearts, we are apt to realize that endings are often the prelude to new beginnings.

—Endings and Beginnings—

When it comes to endings and beginnings, no one can serve as our all-too-human model better than Moses. His story, told in Exodus, is a fascinating journey about never-ending possibilities. Moses, at eighty years old, is comfortable in his ways. He's established a stable, predictable, relatively tranquil life, which is in sharp contrast to his earlier years. But God has more in store.

Moses was born to slave parents in Egypt at a particularly dreadful time for Hebrew mothers. Male babies were to be destroyed, an effort by the pharaoh to halt the growth of the Hebrew population. But Moses's mother, unable to put her little baby to death, put him in a basket and floated him down the Nile, hoping he would be spared. In a wonderful gift of providence, one of the household ladies of Pharaoh's daughter discovered the child. She fell in love with the little Hebrew baby and raised him in her own household as her own, where he received a formal Egyptian education.

When he was a young adult, Moses climbed the ladder of Egyptian success but couldn't shake his Hebrew roots. Once while defending a Hebrew from persecution, Moses took the life of an Egyptian and had no choice but to flee. Eventually he crossed the Nile and wound up on the Sinai Peninsula.

After a time of wilderness wandering, Moses was taken into the household of a Midian priest named Jethro. Eventually Moses married his daughter, established his own family, and was secure and successful. The years went by, and then the decades. Moses had become a permanent part of that Midianite family—stable and successful. But he had entered the final third of his life. To use our modern nomenclature, he was in the third age.

—A Divine Surprise for Moses—

A popular hotel chain used to have the slogan "The best surprise is no surprise." It's catchy and even inviting to those traveling who need a clean, predictable, and comfortable place to spend the night. But it's not necessarily a worthy motto for our lives, especially for those in the third stage of life. In truth, in the third stage of life there are surprises that literally turn our lives around. It's not likely to be a burning bush, but we can begin to feel something warming up within us. This can be especially true in the lives of those who are nearing retirement or who have retired.

Moses got a surprise that would change his life forever. He saw a burning bush. There were probably not many bushes on the side of that barren mountain. Even so, he had never seen one on fire. And not only was the bush burning, it *wasn't* burning to ashes but remained completely in flames!

If you were a spectator to this amazing event, you too would wonder how a bush could catch fire in such a barren place. But then it hits you, the mystery of it all. What could this mean? What could it mean for Moses? What could it mean for you?

As the book of Exodus tells the story, "Moses was keeping the flock of his father-in-law, Jethro, the priest of Midian, and he led his flock beyond the wilderness of Horeb, the mountain of God." God's subtle guiding hand brought Moses to an unfamiliar place. There, Moses found "a bush was blazing, yet it was not consumed." When he dared to look, "God called to him out of the bush, 'Moses, Moses.' And [Moses] said, 'Here I am.'" Consider this: God led Moses, and Moses followed. God spoke to Moses, and Moses, though frightened, listened and replied. Here was a new beginning. God was starting again, and so was Moses. God gave Moses a new job, one that the elderly sheepherder could scarcely believe. The God of Abraham, Isaac, and Jacob had heard the cries of his people enslaved in Egypt. He had chosen Moses to confront Pharaoh and to bring his people out of Egypt. Quite a challenge for one who had been living a comfortable later life! (Exodus 3:1–10)

While this is an ancient story in an unfamiliar setting, some items *are* similar to our stories in today's world. For instance, the burning bush doesn't burn itself up. It's a picture of an inner spiritual surprise all of us could face in the final third of life. The inner prompting of the Spirit within a person, often symbolized in the Bible by fire, doesn't burn itself out. It may be but a whisper in your inner self,

> *The burning bush is a spiritual parable. God may be asking you to consider a new purpose for the rest of your life.*

but it doesn't go away. The bush that is burning but not burning up is a picture, a symbol, a spiritual parable, if you will, that God may be asking you to consider a purpose for the rest of your life.

Self-discoveries often happen at unexpected times. That's what happened to Moses on the slopes of Mount Sinai. Whether we have actually retired or are just considering it, some of life will continue just as it always did. But then something sneaks into our consciousness. We may consider it for a brief while, but then we return to our ordinary routines. Like that bush that was burning so long ago, it refuses to burn itself out. It has to do with what we're supposed to be doing with the rest of our lives.

> *That inner burning bush has to do with the meaning and purpose of our future.*

Dr. Robert Morris, a distinguished sociologist and gerontologist, made many contributions to the understanding of what it means to grow older. When Morris was in his late eighties, Robert Weiss and Scott Bass invited him to contribute a chapter for their book, *Challenges of the Third Age*. Morris's wife, Sara, took seriously ill. He found new purpose in his own life through taking care of her. He cooked her meals, helped her dress, and helped her in and out of her wheelchair.

When Sarah passed away, Morris experienced deep grief. Through his grief, he reflected on something that had happened to him through this chapter in his life. He found that her need for him and his need for her gave him an ongoing sense of purpose.

Morris wrote that two themes still had great power after his experiences with his wife: "One is that life has, or can have, a direction and a purpose, and that a purpose most of us can share is that of making life better. A second, an equally important theme, is that central in whatever we do should be concern for the fates of others—for the fates of our families and neighbors and also of the stranger, the helpless, and the different. A positive and contented life can be found in cherishing how much individuals need each other."[3]

—*Similarities*—

So what does a Moses story hundreds, even thousands, of years old have to do with today's complex world?

First, notice that the repurposing adventure of Moses's life begins not in a religious cathedral but during the normal routine of everyday life. This is often the same pattern God has used through the ages—vibrating through our inner consciousness in an unusual way but in usual circumstances. Some remarkable breakthroughs may happen later, but the whispered call to repurpose life usually breaks into our lives during the routine of daily living.

A *second* similarity between Moses and us is that *helping others* may be a critical component to the repurposing of life. This is in rhythm with the findings of modern sociology and gerontology, and echoes what Dr. Morris discovered about caring for others.

Third, though Moses was eighty years old, there was a lot of life and possibility left in him, and anyone in their later years. Even though he was doing what he could do quite well, there were some personal gifts of leadership that had never been given the opportunity to surface until his later years. What he needed was the same thing many of us need: a *repurposing* of life.

A *fourth* similarity between Moses and us is that God is not going to ask us to do what we cannot do. An important part of *repurposing* your life is to pay attention to the raw materials God gives you throughout the years. Those talents and abilities probably guided you in choosing a profession or calling. And they're still there. In *repurposing* your life, you understand who you are and what you've been able to do with your life. *This is crucially important.* All of your talents and gifts are still present. Lean on them. Call them up. Rejoice in them. God wants to use them not only for your sake, but to encourage others.

Moses was old enough to lead others with maturity and patience. Furthermore, he possessed all of the skills needed. He didn't think he could do it, but God knew he could. God believed in Moses more than Moses believed in himself.

> *It's possible that you can do more than you think you can.*

The encouraging thing to fasten down is **God knew Moses needed a purpose**. Even though Moses was older, God knew there was some real energy left within Moses's mind, soul, and body. In other words, we may be retired and on Social Security—but we are not yet burned out! As Moses was about to find out, God was calling him to repack his bags for a new purpose.

—*The Protests from Within*—

Your response to the *repurposing* of your life may be anything but enthusiastic. Exploring new territory may not be where you are. In this, you and Moses share some common ground. He had no inclination to leave what he was doing and embark upon some new adventure—some new calling—with which he had no experience.

Moses wasted no time beginning a litany of *objections* explaining why he could *not* proceed with God's plan for his later life. In Exodus, chapters 3 and 4, Moses levels with God why he can't go back to Egypt and lead the Jewish people out of bondage and to the Promised Land. He insists there are obvious reasons why this cannot happen, four major objections.

Objection One:

"Who am I that I should go to Pharaoh, and bring the people of Israel out of Egypt?" (Exodus 3:11 GW)

> *Whoever you are or whatever you have been through, you are never too old or too bruised to be about finding the purpose God has for your life.*

Put yourself in Moses's place. He hasn't been near Egypt in decades. Egypt and the pharaoh are in the distant past. He has no knowledge of who in his generation is still alive. His parents have doubtless passed on. Furthermore, he has no experience in what God is asking him to do. Shepherding sheep is a far cry from shepherding a nation of complaining people across a desert.

Suppose you should get an inner nudge about the repurposing of your life. Your first response might be the same as Moses: *Who am I that I should attempt to do that? I'm no longer young.* Or, *I have no experience in that area.* Or, *I've never done that before.* Most of us have said those things—out loud or to ourselves.

To combat those negative reactions, I suggest you think of Harrison Higgins Sr., of Richmond, Virginia. Higgins is an amazing old-fashioned craftsman. He makes handmade furniture built to last. But what's more, he *restores* antique furniture. He's able to see the potential in a piece that on first sight had seen better days, particularly a valuable antique. Where others might see something old and in the way, Higgins sees new possibilities. That old and bruised piece simply needed the careful touch of a master who could make it look new—even better than new![4]

This is a parable about life and its purposes. Sometimes what we need is to see ourselves as candidates for a new beginning, a *repurposing* if you will. We may need to put ourselves in the hands of a Master who can teach us not only to survive, but also to thrive. Often the refashioning of our lives begins with a repurposing. We may not know the answer to that *repurposing* of our lives, but God can help us find it.

Objection Two:

"Moses replied to God, 'Suppose I go to the people of Israel and tell them, 'The God of your ancestors has sent me to you,' and they ask me 'What is his name?' What should I tell them?" (Exodus 3:13 GW)

We can hardly blame Moses for voicing this objection. We've all been there—in need of a letter of introduction, of a name we might drop when interviewing for a job. Moses had a point. After all, who among the Israelites in Egypt would believe him? What if he really did return and tell the long-enslaved Israelites that he had come to lead them out of bondage? Imagine the slaves' responses: *Who did you say sent you? Who are you, again? If you're supposed to be our deliverer, where have you been? We've been in slavery a long time. Who did you say your God was?*

God's answer to Moses was both surprising and emphatic: "I Am Who I Am ... You must tell the people of Israel, 'I Am has sent me to you" (Exodus 3: 14 GW).

In effect, God tells Moses: "Your objection won't hold up. I am God. I have a job for you. Do you really think I can't overcome the problems you encounter?" More important, God reminds Moses that He is the God of Abraham, Isaac, and Jacob. God is saying, "I found a purpose for Abraham, Isaac, and Jacob in their later lives. What makes you think I can't find a purpose for you during the final third of your life?"

Objection Three:

"'They will never believe me or listen to me!' Moses protested ... Then the Lord asked him, 'What's that in your hand?' [Moses] answered, 'A shepherd's staff.' The Lord said, 'Throw it on the ground.' When Moses threw it on the ground, it became a snake." When God told Moses to pick it up, the snake turned into a staff again (Exodus 4:1-4 GW).

These verses are not about the snake but about the staff. God asks, *"What's that in your hand."* God doesn't ask us to do what we can't do. In those days, a staff was a like a shepherd's extra limb. It was a vital part of who they were.

God doesn't ask us to do that for which we have no background. Nor does he ask us to accomplish that for which we have no giftedness, no talent, and no connection. "What's that in your hand," God asked Moses. It's a question for us to ask ourselves. *What is it that you do that is uniquely you? What are your gifts? What experiences can you now put to use in the repurposing of your life?*

It's likely you will find the repurposing of your life will involve some interest or ability that you already possess. It will just be used in ways you never expected.

There's great symbolism here. "What is in your hand, Moses?" God doesn't demand of us what we don't have. He wants to use what's already there, like a staff to a shepherd.

Objection Four:

This is more a plea than an objection. "Please, Lord, send somebody else." (Exodus 4:13 GW)

The obvious, but painful, truth about this objection is that we've all been there, wishing to transfer our responsibilities to the shoulders of someone else. But in the *repurposing* of our lives, the genius of what God is doing with us is making our future meaningful and significant. Without His personal touch, we forfeit the joy in fulfilling our future destiny. We would forfeit the joy of being at the right place at the right time with the right purpose on behalf of others.

—*From Survive to Thrive*—

Moses's purpose in life during his earlier years was to survive. He had fled Egypt many decades ago with no hope, no direction—in essence, no future. But he

> *Thriving means we believe we've come as far as we have for a greater purpose than survival.*

was a survivor. He had made a life for himself. He had a home, a family, and a career. Likely, he looked forward to putting his feet up on the couch and maybe even taking naps in the afternoon! Moses was indeed a true survivor.

But there is something better than simply surviving. Our spiritual lives are so much richer when we move from merely surviving to thriving. We need to accept that life with a significant purpose is a higher step than simply surviving. As Craig McBean and Henry Simmons stated in *Thriving Beyond Midlife*, "The further one gets from midlife, the more the need for individual and conscious goal setting. Waiting to die—a strategy for many folks—does not support thriving."[5]

> *Our lives need a purpose and a meaning that will allow us to thrive personally and spiritually, perhaps more deeply than any other time of life.*

Eventually Moses gave himself to the purpose God had for him. He set out for Egypt. With the help of the ten plagues and a miracle or two, it happened. The Exodus, the escape from Egypt, happened. Eventually, Moses led the Hebrew people to their homeland, the Promised Land, the land of Abraham, Isaac, and Jacob. That homeland gave birth to people who are still speaking to us, such as David, Solomon, Isaiah, Jesus and his disciples, and many others.

—What about You?—

Suppose you set out to *repurpose* your life. From the start, be patient with yourself. Decisions come hard. You may be at the process stage, not the quick decision stage. Like Tennyson's verse in "Ulysses" about one's mature years, "Though much is taken, much abides ... that which we are, we are."[6]

Consider another very important point: Like Moses, you may need to develop your ability to listen and perceive through your prayer life. "Lord, give me what you have made me to want, and grant me what you have made me long for."

> God has built into us a longing for something that the world can't give us, a purpose for living and thriving.

Perhaps Moses's greatest prayer appears in Psalm 90:

Lord, you have been our dwelling place in all generations,
Before the mountains were brought
forth, or ever you had formed
   The earth and the world,
From everlasting to everlasting you are God ...
For a thousand years in your sight are but as yesterday
when it is past, or as a watch in the night. ...
So teach us to count our days that we
may gain a wise heart. ...
Satisfy us in the morning with your steadfast love,
   so that we may rejoice and be glad all our days.
...
Let the favor of the Lord our God be upon us,
   And prosper for us the work of our hands;
   Yes, prosper the work of our hands! (Psalms 90:1–17)

—*The Honeyguide Bird*—

Return again to Richard Leider and his experience with the Hazda tribe in the East African nation of Tanzania. Recall that a huge fire had been built in honor of those on the walking safari. They were invited to sit in places of honor closest to the fire built on their behalf.

On that night, an elder of the tribe, Maroba, rose to tell the story his people had heard countless times about the honeyguide bird, a small gray- and rust-colored bird about the size of a robin. It gets its name from its function. It leads them to honey, upon which their lives depend.

Maroba reminded the tribe to keep their eyes and ears open for the honeyguide bird wherever they go. When they hear the *"wee-teer, wee-teer"* of the bird, they must whistle back. Then the bird will lead them to the bee's nest, which is dripping with honey.

> *What we need in life is available to us only if we know how to look for it.*

Later, as Leider considered the story, he realized that it exposed a basic truth about all of life. *What we need in life is available to us only if we know how to look for it.* Along with his co-author, David Shapiro, he has written an insightful book, *Claiming Your Place at the Fire: Living the Second Half of your Life*, on what it means to be an elder in our kind of world. They ask, what is it that enables us, in our culture, to sit closest to the fire in our later years, instead of being lost in the shadows of retirement?[7]

For Leider and Shapiro, four key questions determine what to look for in finding our purpose in our later years. These four questions reflect the story of Moses and God's call to *repurpose* his life and are, in a sense, *our* honeyguide birds:

1. Who am I?
2. Where do I belong?
3. What do I care about?
4. What is my life's purpose?

Of these four, the one that will surface most often in the writings of sociologists and gerontologists is the question about meaning and purpose in our later years. How do we discern our purposes in life when parents, teachers, coaches, and vocation no longer dictate what and who we are? Answering the four questions listed above can be like a honeyguide bird for us. They also help us move beyond the objections Moses gave before he finally moved forward with God's purpose for the rest of his life.

When examining the life of Moses, what other questions should we be asking ourselves?

- **What is God calling me to be and to do in this stage of my life?**
- **Am I willing to be patient and listen through my prayer life to discover what the next steps are for me?**

CHAPTER 2

The Barnabas Discovery:
A Gift Hidden in Plain Sight

*May our Lord Jesus Christ himself and
God our Father, who loved us and by his
grace gave us eternal encouragement and
good hope, encourage your hearts and
strengthen you in every good deed and word.*
—2 Thessalonians 2:16–17 NIV

The Barnabas Discovery

A Gift Hidden in Plain Sight

Os Guinness, the author and social commentator, tells a story about a furniture factory in communist Russia. The factory made lovely furniture, yet so many of the workers lived in poverty that stealing had become an epidemic. Soon, guards were put at every exit hoping to deter additional theft. One day a worker exited the factory with a wheelbarrow full of sawdust and shavings. A suspicious guard stopped the worker and inquired, "What do you have in that wheelbarrow, comrade?"

The answer: "Oh, there's nothing in here but sawdust and shavings."

"Dump it out," said the guard. Sure enough, there was nothing in that wheelbarrow but sawdust and shavings.

This encounter and conversation went on day after day with the same outcome: the same questions, the same answers, the same dumping out of the sawdust on the floor. Finally the guard could stand it no more. He said to the worker, "Look, I know you're stealing. You know you're stealing. If you tell me what you are stealing, I promise I won't arrest you."

"You promise you won't arrest me?" the worker asked.

"I promise," came back the reply.

The worker paused, looked the guard full in the face, and with a smile said, "Wheelbarrows, comrade. Wheelbarrows." A secret hidden in plain sight! Encouragement can be like that: *a gift hidden in plain sight.*[1]

William Barclay once said, "One of the highest of human duties is the duty of encouragement. … It is easy to laugh at man's ideals. It's easy to pour cold water on enthusiasm. It's easy to discourage others—the world is full of discouragers."[2] On a spiritual level, encouragement is one of those secrets in plain sight. Almost everyone is in favor of encouragement, but when spiritual gifts are mentioned almost all of the others would be listed ahead of encouragement in order of importance. Diane Milnes, in her book *Be An Encourager*, suggests that we need at least ten times as many encouragers as we do people with other spiritual gifts.[3]

—Encouragement in the Bible—

Travel in your mind to the Old Testament story about David, roughly 1000 BC, or 3,000 years ago. King Saul is jealous of, and threatened by, this handsome young warrior named David. Fearing for his life, David hides in the hills. Then the scripture springs a surprise.

While trying to hide in the desert, David received a visit from none other than Saul's son, Jonathan. *God helped Jonathan encourage David.* "Don't be afraid," Jonathan said, "My father Saul will never get his hands on you. In fact, *you're going to be the next king of Israel"* (1 Samuel 23:15-17 CEV, emphasis mine).

What Jonathan said would happen, did happen, largely because Jonathan believed in David. But what's even more fascinating is that the Bible speaks about *God encouraging David through Jonathan.* This is before Saul became king, before the ninety Psalms were attributed to David. This is a thousand years before the church was born. God has been encouraging his people through others from the beginning.

> *"But the Counselor, the **Holy Spirit,** whom the Father will send in my name, will teach you all things and will remind you of everything I have said to you."*
>
> —John 14:26 NIV

Fast forward to the earliest days of the church, almost a thousand years after David. In those days, Jewish males were required to go to Jerusalem for one of the three main Jewish festivals: Yom Kippur (in the fall), Passover (early spring), or Pentecost (late spring). This was a requirement for faithful Jewish men regardless of where one lived.

One who arrived in Jerusalem from Cyprus during the festival of Pentecost was a Jewish man named Joseph. Joseph from Cyprus? Most of us are familiar with two biblical Josephs—the Old Testament boy with the coat of many colors and the New Testament Joseph, husband of Mary, the mother of Jesus. But most of us have never heard of this *third* Joseph.

There's good reason for our lacking knowledge about the other Joseph: the early church changed his name. They came to love Joseph. He believed in them. He encouraged them. They observed him. Then they renamed him Barnabas, Son of Encouragement. Although never called Joseph again, Barnabas is mentioned in the New Testament twenty-five times in the chapters of Acts and four times in Paul's letters. His name change was permanent and descriptive. The Holy Spirit was doing through Barnabas the same thing the Spirit was doing a thousand years before through Saul's son, Jonathan.

The Greek word *paraklatos* found in John 14:26 describes the Holy Spirit. It is translated in various ways: *counselor, comforter, helper,* and sometimes

> *Jonathan and Barnabas knew about the indispensable power that occurs when one person believes in another and encourages them.*

simply with English letters *paraclete.* The Greek word for Barnabas is *paralaseos* (Acts 4:36), which is very similar. They come from the same root word. Only the endings are different. Both have to do with believing in encouragement. The early

Christians described Barnabas and the Holy Spirit by the same root word. They knew about the indispensable power that occurs when one person believes in another and encourages them.

Barnabas and Jonathan lived a thousand years apart, but the Spirit of God used both of them to strengthen and guide others. Why is this important for us? Because the same Spirit that was at work through Jonathan three thousand years ago and then through Barnabas two thousand years ago is at work in you and me today.

—Believing in Someone—

How does one come to believe in another person and encourage them?

One of the key factors in the hidden dynamic of encouragement is whether one person really believes in the worth of another. Barnabas was called to believe in others, one of whom was Saul of Tarsus, later the Apostle Paul. Many were afraid of Saul. Others doubted his sincerity. Still others rejected him completely. But Barnabas believed in him in spite of what others were saying. Barnabas must've known that great faith comes not because we are sure of ourselves, but rather because we trust that *God is sure of us*. And through everything that happens, God is not going to let us go. When we believe in others and encourage them, we plant this seed in others.

One of the hidden factors woven into confidence and self-assurance is one we seldom express. It's the difference it makes when someone really believes in us. The issues we face, the disappointments we live through, are visible to many but not often mentioned. We deal with them as best we can. Mostly we stew about them. Others are mostly shut out. We see ourselves as our own counselor, coach, guide, and helper. It's all kept inside. Eventually we begin to withdraw, sometimes almost completely.

Who are we called to encourage?

Michael Yaconelli was a remarkable person. He had an unusual way of speaking about his faith. On occasion his presentations were a bit strong and frank for some people. He sometimes used phrases not often employed by a well-known Christian speaker.

He frequently told stories focused on the power of encouragement. One of them was about Dr. Lorraine Monroe, who for many years

> Encouragers are indispensable amidst the tensions and troubles of today's world.

taught high school students in Harlem. One year in her advanced English class sat a very bright student who had shown great promise. But in his senior year, his grades nose-dived. She met with the boy, threatened him, challenged him, and encouraged him, all to no avail. At the end of the year, the young man barely passed. Dr. Monroe sadly marked this as another casualty of the urban jungle.

One morning ten years later, Dr. Monroe was walking to work when a well-dressed young man approached her. It turned out to be this same young man she taught so many years ago. Asked if she recognized him, she quickly responded and said she remembered him so well because he had so much promise but had wasted it.

His reply was not what she expected. "I knew you believed in me even though you were disappointed in my performance. I've always hoped I'd run into you again so I could thank you for believing in me because I am now one of the editorial writers for *Time Magazine*, and I owe much of my success to you. You see, Dr. Monroe, my senior year was a difficult year for my family. My father was in prison, my mother was a prostitute, my older brother was selling drugs in the projects, and I was left to care for my younger sister and brother. Dr. Monroe, 70 percent was all I could give you!"[4]

—*"You Can Do This, You Know"*—

That young man was giving the best he could—*under the circumstances*. He was still giving his best. And that is what we must give—for others and for ourselves. It takes time, and it takes support, but we can move from despair and isolation to engagement and community.

Once I gave a talk to the residents of a retirement community, and afterward I met a woman—let's call her Hazel—who told me an unforgettable story about her own difficult transition. Let me share her story.

Hazel walked slowly into her new life—a resident in a retirement community. She had not wanted to move from her home of many years. Yes, it really was for the best, given her health needs. But she moved to the retirement community with reluctance, even a sense that she had somehow been betrayed. No amount of sparkle, bells, or service-with-a-smile would have made this move an enthusiastic one. Upon arrival, she basically withdrew from everyone. Hazel didn't lock her door, but she never invited anyone to her place. For all practical purposes, she locked both her door and her heart to outsiders.

Then one of the other residents—her name was Fran—took it upon herself to intervene. It was not easy, for it was clear to Fran that her frequent visits were not welcome. Most residents would have given up at that point, but Fran persisted. She would stop by Hazel's room and talk about the day, the opportunities, and what was going on in the world. Then before leaving, she would say, "You can do this, you know. You can make this transition. I know it's hard. It was hard for me. But you can do it. I know you can."

Fran would often invite Hazel to have lunch or dinner, or to attend some opportunity offered at the retirement community. The invitation was always refused.

Then one day, to Fran's surprise, the silent and isolated Hazel accepted her invitation to have dinner. It wasn't easy for Hazel to break her withdrawal tendencies, but it started, she told me, with Fran's invitations and her own little "yes." Little by little, the walls she had built around her heart came down, and Hazel, a pint-sized resident in unfamiliar surroundings, reentered her world. Slowly, she began venturing out on her own—quietly exploring her new home.

One day she chose to attend a lecture. I was giving that lecture, and my subject on that particular morning had to do with believing in one's self. The basic message was to encourage the residents to make a difference in their world, even though they were up in years.

After it was over, Hazel waited until I had spoken to others who had come by after the service. As she began to tell me her story, the tears came. Obviously she was dealing with a most important chapter in her life. When she finished, she summarized as if she had been practicing. She said, "To believe in yourself you have to first of all have someone to believe in you. That is what Fran did for me. She believed in me even when I didn't believe in myself and even when I didn't want her to believe in me."

*It was one of those quiet, poignant moments when nothing needed to be said. I nodded and then reached out and gave her a hug. But Hazel wasn't quite finished. She repeated what she had already said, but she said it again as if it were the summary of her life right then: "**To believe in yourself, even to believe in God, you have to have someone really believe in you.**"*

Believing in yourself and others, in their worth, in their possibilities, is an essential basic foundation for encouragement. Can you have the perceptiveness and patience of Fran? Yes, you can, and it can make all the difference in someone else's life. Can you finally find the courage to say yes to an invitation? Hazel found that courage, and so can you. That is the Barnabas discovery.

—Encouragement Is Part of Love—

Another element woven into the dynamic of encouragement is the strong cable of love. St. Paul makes it the strongest cable of all to the Corinthian believers: "Now faith, hope, and love abide, these three; and the greatest of these is love" (I Corinthians 13:13). Perhaps it's more correct to see encouragement as one of the strong cables that make love real and personal.

In the well-known and beloved book, *Chicken Soup for the Soul*, the significant impact a little encouragement can have on the people in our lives is conveyed through a story contributed by Eric Butterworth:

A college professor had his sociology class go into the Baltimore slums to get case histories of 200 young boys. They were asked to write an evaluation of each boy's future. In every case the students wrote, "He hasn't got a chance." Twenty-five years later another sociology professor came across the earlier study. He had his students follow up on the project to see what had happened to these boys. With the exception of 20 boys who had moved away or died, the students learned that 176 of the remaining 180 had achieved more than ordinary success as lawyers, doctors and businessmen.

The professor was astounded and decided to pursue the matter further. He was able to ask each one, "How do you account for your success?" In each case the reply came with feeling, "There was a teacher."

The teacher was still alive, so he sought her out and asked the old-but-still-alert lady what magic formula she had used to pull these boys out of the slums into successful achievement?

The teacher's eyes sparkled and her lips broke into a gentle smile. "It's really very simple," she said. "I loved those boys."[5]

Had we asked those early Christians in Jerusalem how Barnabas the Encourager helped them survive, what might they have said? It might have gone like this: "Well, you see, there was this encourager, Barnabas, who really believed in us and loved us. He sold some land and gave us money so we could eat. He loved us, and encouraged us, and kept telling us we could make it, and we did. In fact, we changed his name from Joseph to Barnabas—because the name Barnabas means *son of encouragement*!

Encouragement's Bigger Picture: We May Never Know Our Part

Almost everyone has heard of St. Paul. Not many realize had it not been for Barnabas, there might never have been an apostle named Paul. Paul (originally Saul) was born in Tarsus. His parents sent him to the best schools, and when he was old enough, they sent him to Jerusalem to the seminary.

Then Jesus appeared on the scene. He was a threat to Jerusalem's religious establishment. He taught not in synagogues but on street corners. He welcomed not only good folks but also tax collectors and even prostitutes to hear him. He was also a healer. Some of the things he did were not only miraculous, they'd never been done before.

Saul of Tarsus was an enemy of the faith Jesus talked about. When Jesus was crucified, Saul rejoiced. But then came reports that Christ had risen from the dead. Saul scoffed at it all. *Absurd!*

Nonsense! Then, at Pentecost, one of Jesus's followers, Simon Peter, preached, and hundreds responded. They wanted to know more. Many were baptized. Saul was aghast—this nonsense was spreading. He volunteered to do whatever he could to stamp out this heresy.

Saul was successful in his relentless persecution of Jesus's followers. He never saw a Christian he didn't want to get rid of. So they sent him to put down a growing set of believers in

> *These were radical times when perhaps the best example of rock-your-world/upset-the-apple-cart change happened.*

Damascus. But on the road to Damascus, something happened that turned his life around. As the story goes in chapter 9 of the Book of Acts, a bright light from heaven, like a spotlight, shone upon him, and he heard a voice, "Saul, Saul, why do you persecute me?"

"Who are you, Lord?" Saul replied.

"I am Jesus, who you are persecuting. But rise. Stand to your feet. I will show you where to go." He was sent to the home of Ananias, a brave believer, and Saul came to believe that Jesus was the Messiah, the Christ (Acts 9:4–6).

Saul went back to Jerusalem, but he was different. He fit nowhere. The Pharisees realized he was a changed man and shunned him. The Christians were still scared to death of him.

There was, however, one early believer who reached out to Saul. That's right! It was Barnabas, who put his arm around Saul and welcomed him as a brother in Christ. Yet the bulk of believers remained afraid, and Saul's former allies were angry at his change of heart, so he gave up and went home to Tarsus—a changed man, but an outcast.

Meanwhile, believers in Antioch were increasing, and they sent word to the church in Jerusalem that they needed a teacher. None of the church leaders was eager to go to Antioch, but they knew of a man who had the means to travel and the right personality. They sent Barnabas to Antioch to build up the church there (Acts 11:20–26).

From Antioch to Tarsus and Back Again

Antioch welcomed Barnabas with open arms. He gave his witness. He shared his faith and the story of Jesus Christ. He shared about the crucifixion and resurrection. He shared his own story of being raised in Crete and his conversion during the Pentecost feast at Jerusalem.

When the new believers in Antioch asked questions, particularly about the Jewish scriptures, Barnabas wasn't able to help much. He'd never been to rabbinical school. There was no New Testament yet, so he could not point to that. His vocation was probably in real estate, not theology. Barnabas realized he needed help. He needed Saul.

Not long before, Saul had needed Barnabas. Now Barnabas needed Saul. Trained as a Hebrew rabbi, Saul had a deep knowledge of the scripture. He would be able to explain Christ's salvation to the people of Antioch from a scriptural viewpoint. The believers there did not know that Saul had formerly persecuted Christians, so they wouldn't fear him! So Barnabas left for Tarsus—a "people person" in search of an exiled scholar.

Barnabas goes to Antioch to new believers who are in need of a teacher	Barnabas travels to Tarsus to encourage Saul (Paul)	Barnabas brought Paul back to Antioch, where they teach together

Tarsus was a huge city, but Barnabas persisted, found Saul, and brought him back to Antioch.

For a year and a half Barnabas and Saul built a foundation under the faith of those new believers. It was there that Saul made clear to believers that the life, death, and resurrection of Jesus, the son of God, was rooted and foretold in the ancient Hebrew scriptures. Most important, Saul came to understand what he was to do with the rest of his life. God had called him to be a proclaimer of the Gospel, a teacher, an evangelist, a missionary.

Eventually, Saul of Tarsus would change his name to Paul—a name that signified the change from his old life to his new life and, because Paul was an identifiably Gentile name, signified the essential point that Christianity was a faith open to all.[6]

Paul would become a leader of the New Testament church and indeed became the author of thirteen of the twenty-seven books in our New Testament.

> *For Saul to become Paul, he needed someone who believed in him and encouraged him. Oh the difference an encourager makes!*

What if there had never been a Barnabas who embraced Saul after the Damascus Road? What if Barnabas had not believed in Saul's potential? What if Barnabas had never encouraged the outcast believer, had never placed him in a position to utilize his intellectual gifts?

Here is a crucial lesson that applies to later life. For Saul to become Paul, he needed someone who believed in him and encouraged him. Oh the difference an encourager makes!

—An Encourager Believes in the Potential in Others—

While Barnabas and Paul were in Antioch, the believers in Jerusalem were suffering a great deal. One of those believers was his young nephew, John Mark. Eventually, Mark would move to Antioch, which is where he met Paul. The encourager Barnabas might have been distraught to find that his protégé, Paul, and his faithful nephew, Mark, did not always see eye to eye.

One scholar, Robert L. Cate, author of *One Untimely Born*, has stated that Paul and Mark disagreed on Paul's mission strategy. When the three left Antioch to go on their first mission trip, Paul thought it best to cover as much ground as possible. The three would stay a few weeks in one place then move on. According to Cate, Mark disagreed. Mark, who later became Peter's amanuensis, thought that each church needed teaching, training, and written works to provide guidance. The trouble was, as Mark saw it, Paul and Barnabas left a place with nothing but their memories of Paul and Barnabas. Mark wanted to stay longer and plant roots. Perhaps Paul and Mark exchanged angry words.[7]

> *Encouragement does something other than encourage. It opens up possibilities.*

Perhaps it is useful to remember that good works and ministry—like later life itself—are seldom all sweetness and light, even with a Barnabas at hand. A touch of realism helps.

At any rate, Mark left his elders and returned to Antioch. The next time Paul and Mark argued, Barnabas took Mark's side of the argument and left for home: Cyprus. At that point, Barnabas and Mark drop out of Luke's account in the book of Acts, and we hear no more of them. What we do know is that Mark followed up on his desire to provide written materials as a foundation of Christian faith. He wrote his Gospel.

What is lost in all of these discussions is that Barnabas came to believe in Mark's point of view. And eventually Paul did, too!

Out of this debate will come the letters we have in the New Testament to provide instruction for those young churches. In what may be his last letter, Paul asks his

> *"Anxiety weighs down the human heart, but a good word cheers it up."*
> —Proverbs 12:25

readers to tell Mark to come to his side in prison because Mark would be *"profitable to me."* It's Paul's way of saying, "I didn't see it then, but I see it now."

Part of the reason we have Mark's Gospel in the New Testament is because Barnabas kept encouraging his younger nephew to write. Mark kept records of what Peter preached. Mark's Gospel has sometimes been called Peter's Gospel, because some believe that Mark simply recorded what Peter preached and taught. That may be a stretch, but Mark was one of those sharp young minds the Lord reaches in all generations.

—*Encouragement*—

Encouragement is often overlooked in a world that usually defines success in terms of fast-paced productivity and results. Yet many who achieve success in any given endeavor give credit to someone who believed in and encouraged them along the way. For example, every four years the Olympic Games roll around. Winners

> *Encouragement is often overlooked in a world that usually defines success in terms of rapid results.*

are endlessly interviewed. The interviews are amazingly similar from one Olympics to the next. The winners, some of whom will have broken records long ago set, often with deep gratitude give most credit to someone who encouraged them along the way. Instead of mentioning the many hours of training or the abilities that enabled them to succeed, they bring attention to the people who encouraged them. It might have been their parents, coaches, spouses, or teammates. While their incredible skill made their success possible, what surfaces in their interviews is the place encouragement has played in their ability to succeed. It is a huge example of the power of encouragement.

At the end of our lives, most of us would want to be remembered for our convictions. In this respect, we may find ourselves in one of these categories in our later years. There are three kinds of people:

- There are those who are against something most of the time. At the end of life, they are remembered as harsh critics, as joyless souls.
- There are those who are neither hot nor cold, indifferent to life, minding one's own business; they are not remembered much, if at all.
- There are those who believed in others, who built them up and believed in their possibilities. At the end of their life, they are remembered for their encouragement of others.

What about you? Who in your life believed in you, encouraged you in good times and bad, and stood with you as you tried to live out your possibilities? Will you, because of them, believe and encourage others even as you believe in and encourage yourself? This is what Christ does for us.

Even when we didn't believe in Him, not even ourselves, and in fact didn't believe in much of anything, He believed in us. Eventually His believing in us began to make all the difference. What He did for us was an outward expression of what He knew from the beginning—that *we were worth loving and even worth saving*. Eventually we came to believe in Him as well as ourselves.

CHAPTER 3

The Abraham Discovery:
Risk, Regret, and Reward

Now the Lord said to Abram [Abraham],
'Go from your country and your kindred
and your father's house to the land I will
show you. I will make of you a great nation,
and I will bless you, and make your name
great, so that you will be a blessing.'
—Genesis 12:1–2

The Abraham Discovery

Risk, Regret, and Reward

All kinds of firsts are found in the book of Genesis, especially chapters one through eleven—the creation of the cosmos, the beginning of the family, the beginning of choice, and the first rainbow. There's also the first sin, the first murder, and the first dysfunctional family.

Starting in the twelfth chapter of Genesis, a new beginning breaks forth like the sun through the clouds after the storm. God calls Abram to be the beginning of the Jewish people, and the beginning of faith. As the creation of the world begins with God speaking, so the beginning of faith begins with God speaking and Abram listening. Isn't that the way it is with us— God speaking and us listening? In other religions, the trick is to figure out how to get through to God, but in the Bible, that order is turned around. Now the question is, how is God able to get through to us? Like Carlo Caretto states in his book *The God Who Comes,* "God is always coming, and we, like Adam, are called to hear His footsteps."[1] Somehow Abraham was able to rise above what Thomas Cahill, author of the best-selling book

The Gifts of the Jews, called "the civilized repository of the predictable."[2] He learned how to listen. A question for each one of us is this: If God is trying to get my attention, have I learned how to listen to God?

As Abram's story unfolds in the book of Genesis, chapters 12–25, it is clear that the life he lives is far from perfect, but he doesn't miss his calling—God's design for his later life. And it is worth underscoring the point that *when God first speaks to Abram in the book of Genesis, Abram was already seventy-five years old!* Our aging bodies and minds might scare us (and, on occasion, scare our caregivers), but they do not scare God. Time and again in the Bible, God seeks out those in later life and says, "I have something for you to do. Will you do it?" Your calling for later life has arrived. Will you say yes to God?

Abram said yes, and in his new stage of life he took on the name we still use for him: *Abraham.* Today, Abraham is the acknowledged founder of Judaism, Christianity, and Islam. He did not know his "yes" would have such a widespread influence throughout the world. No. He just said yes when God called him, and Abram became Abraham. We do not need to change our names, but we will have choices to make about our later lives.

Abraham died at age one hundred, having followed his later-life calling for a quarter of a century. The story in Genesis suggests he died without regrets. What we do not know, however, is whether he had regrets in his early seventies, when old age was creeping up on him and he had yet to hear God's call to go forth from his home in Haran. "Go from your country and your kindred and your father's house to the land I will show you. I will make of you a great nation, and I will bless you, and make your name great, so that you will be a blessing" (Genesis 12:1–2).

That's quite a calling! Most of us won't be called to make a great nation or to be famous in our later years. But if we listen for our own personal calling, and we act upon it, as Abraham acted on God's call to him, *we can expect to be blessed and to be a blessing to others in need.*

Was Abraham feeling regrets as later life came upon him, in the years just before God called him? We can never know. Most of us do reach later life with regrets—some big, some small. We probably all know a friend, a family member, or a neighbor who has pulled us aside and said, with a pained look, "I feel like I missed out on my own life—and now it's too late." It's tragic to miss your calling, to miss out on your true life because you're too busy to stop and listen for God's quiet message. That kind of regret hurts, really hurts.

But is it really too late? *The Abraham Discovery is God's emphatic answer: It is not too late!* Age is no barrier to a calling for your life—perhaps a calling that is as surprising to you as God's call was to a seventy-five-year-old man so long ago.

—*Lifelong Learning*—

What a fearful thing to think you've lived half of your life waiting for the right time and circumstances in your own mind. Gregg Levoy, author of *Callings: Finding and Following an Authentic Life*, calls boredom "the common cold of the soul." Sometimes it is. But just as common is waking up and realizing you have lived by an agenda that has nothing to do with what you were created to be and do in this season of life.[3]

God has an antidote for that problem. It happens at the very beginning of every life of faith. It happened at the beginning of Abraham's life of faith. It's not at all what we would expect. God sometimes seeks to get through to us in a worship service, or through a Scripture or with a sermon, and sometimes even through a hymn. But God also begins with a call we hear in our innermost spiritual self, often during a quiet time of prayer and meditation. In the Scripture, God sometimes communicates through dreams, or through angels, or, as with Moses, through the drama of a burning bush. But what matters most about Abraham is that, when God sought him out, he was open to what God was asking him to do: to risk a complete break with the family and society he knew to follow God's lead.

—*Overlooking Abraham*—

Many believers have somehow overlooked Abraham. A pastor recalled that as a young boy he missed out on the study of

Abraham. The members of the little church where he grew up in the 1940s and '50s were sure Christ was coming back *any day.* Their primary focus seemed to be not *whether* Christ would return but *when*! Much attention was given to books of prophecy, such as Ezekiel, Daniel, and Revelation. So the young boy—who went on to become a pastor—overlooked Abraham. Many years later, he was reading the book *Fear and Trembling*, by Soren Kierkegaard, and was introduced to Abraham. Since then he's never ceased to be awed.

An often-overlooked aspect of the Abraham story is the kind of person God called to become the father of the Jewish nation. First, he's

> *Abraham was not a preacher or a religious expert. He was a layman.*

not a preacher, a clergyman, a priest, or any other kind of religious professional. He's a layman. So far as we know, he never preached a sermon, taught a lesson, or sang in a choir—certainly not a solo. He was not an expert on the scriptures; there weren't any. He just obeyed God.

Second, he never changed careers. His vocation was that of a herdsman. He was good at it. He created great wealth through it. But this was like the cocoon in which the butterfly of his calling was held and allowed to survive.

Third, though a layman, he wasn't the kind of man who just let his mind wander all over the place while tending his flocks. His mind must have often turned toward questions about God as well as himself. What was his place in the big picture of the world in which he lived? He probably spent time every day pondering the questions of life and purpose. It must have been during one of these times that God came to him and called him to the work he was destined to do.

—The Calling—

Embrace the fact that Abraham was a layman, a rancher, a herdsman, because some people confuse career with calling. You can fulfill your calling in most any career. A person's calling is inevitably fulfilling because it has to do with the personal gifts one has been given. What was Abraham's gift? He could lead. *It's through the gift of leadership that he lived out God's dream for his life.*

How do we know what spiritual gifts we have been given? Sometimes it comes through prayer and meditation. But often we discover our gifts by realizing the things that replenish and restore us. That which blesses us will also serve as a blessing to others.

Even if your career may end with retirement and success, your *calling* isn't over until the day you die. The rewards of your vocation are significant and need

> *You are not a spare part in God's creation. Within your success and failures, God calls forth your gifts to be used for his people.*

49

to be honored. However, they're temporary. Your calling—turning your gifts loose among those you are with—bridges into eternity. A vocation can be interrupted, but a calling never is.

Sometimes a calling develops late in life or even out of a troubled experience. Charles Colson was in President Richard Nixon's administration. He enjoyed one of the most high-profile careers in our national government. He had enormous influence and access to the heart of power. Then Colson landed in prison due to the Watergate scandal. *His career was over, but his calling was just beginning.* While he was in prison, God came to him like He came to Abraham and called him to a special purpose: to give prisoners both his good news and his brokenness. He reflected, "The real legacy of my life was my biggest failure—that I was an ex-convict. My great humiliation—being sent to prison—was the beginning of God's greatest use of my life; He chose the one experience in which I could not glory for His glory."[4]

As you look back at your life, do you see unrealized potential and unfulfilled longings? Do you feel that you've left life behind in the living of it? Consider these lines from a popular poem. Perhaps, with the poet, you also regret:

Lives you never touched,
And you're sitting in a recliner with a shriveled soul,
And forgotten dreams,
And you realize there was a world of desperate need,

And a great God calling you to be part of something bigger
than yourself—
You see the person you could have become but did not;
You never followed your calling.[5]

—The Risk—

Think about Abram—
not yet Abraham. He tells
everyone he has developed
a personal relationship with
God. In doing so, he risked
his status in the community.
A personal relationship with
God? That was something

> As you look at your life, do
> you see unrealized potential
> or unfulfilled longings? Do
> you feel that somehow you've
> left something behind in the
> living of it?

religious people of the day would not have understood. Nor
would family. Nor would friends. They might have said, "I think
our friend Abram, who we love and respect, has something
wrong with him. He thinks he hears from some god somewhere.
I'm worried about his sanity."

The wise men of Abram's day based their understanding of the
world on their study of the stars or a wide assortment of gods.
Along comes Abram saying, in effect, "I have an inner compass
you know nothing about."

Abram was asked to make a complete break with the past. The mainstream viewpoint of his era was that everything was decided by the stars, by the gods, by whatever. Then Abram has a dream of something new, something better, something yet to happen. "So he went," with a promise from his God that, in risking it all to fulfill God's dream for his life, he was right and the others were wrong. From Abram came Abraham. From Abraham came the Jews. From the Jews came Jesus, our Lord. It all began on that day when in his soul, an ordinary and elderly man said yes.

- It's a great risk to say yes to God. But it's a greater risk to say nothing.
- It's a great risk to move into uncomfortable territory. But it's a greater risk to end one's life filled with regret.

—It All Begins with a Yes—

In the final third of our lives, we encounter new and unexpected ways to say yes to God. Is saying yes a risk? You bet. But it is a much bigger risk to stand silently before your potential. The word "yes" may be the most powerful three-letter word in our language. When we say yes to God, we bring together two powerful forces: the power of our affirmation and the power of God's call.

By the way, the New Testament has a single word for *risk*. It is the word *faith*. Abraham gave the world faith. Is there anything sadder than a life that has gone the other direction? Instead of go, there's stay. Instead of risk, there's regret. Instead of a dream, there's a drift.

People in later life will sometimes say, in despair, "I have nothing left to live for." But God would disagree. His calling for you in your final third of life may be vastly different than His calling for you when you were a young adult. But that doesn't make it any less important to God—or to those around you who are in need of the gifts you have to offer. Have faith and take a risk. Say yes to your new calling.

CALLED

To let loose our gifts upon the world

To be used by God in His world that needs His touch

CHAPTER 4

The Paul Discovery:
The Divine Hush of Fear Not

*Being confident of this,
that He who began a good work in you
will carry it on to completion
until the day of Christ Jesus.*
—Philippians 1:6 NIV

The Paul Discovery

The Divine Hush of Fear Not

Except for a leap year, there are 365 days in our yearly calendar. This is also the number of times that fear is mentioned in the Bible—which might suggest that fear is a daily proposition, even for people of faith.

Truth is, we've lived a lot, seen a lot, and it's true—the things we see and hear in our world, and face ourselves, can create a spirit of fear. Paul would encourage us to face them head-on. To learn to trust, we must face the gravity of our fears. They can have great power. Think of the potential power from the perspective of a process definition of fear. Fear is a reaction to a feeling. So, in addition to basic survival fear, are there some deep, abiding fears living within us? *What do we do with these deep, abiding fears?*

In Acts 27, authored by Luke, we get an account of the Apostle Paul overcoming fear in the midst of an awful storm. Luke must have come to visit Paul at Caesarea and was now making the journey back home with him. As he was setting sail for home, the first leg of the journey went well, but then the winds turned and "we sailed slowly for a number of days" (Acts 27:7). Paul, who had incredible discernment, knew that much time had been lost and warned them to put up for the winter. But Julius, the Roman centurion, following the advice of the pilot of the ship, set sail.

Luke lets us know that during the storm, the crew jettisoned all kinds of essentials. They threw overboard what earlier they would have considered indispensable. First the cargo was thrown overboard. Then it was over the side with the ship's tackle. Finally they even threw the grain over (Acts 27:18–19, 38).

This was a journey where nothing seemed to be going right. That night, an angel came to Paul with

> *Trusting in God is a major step in overcoming your fears.*

a message (Acts 27:21–26). The next day, Paul made quite a speech to the terrified crew. He told them of the angel and its message—that no one on board would die, though the ship itself would break apart on an island. Some of them probably believed him and some didn't. On the fourteenth night, some sailors began to sense they were nearing land. The waves pounded the ship; fearing they would be dashed upon the rocks, the crew put down all the anchors in desperation.

Then just before dawn, Paul did an incredible thing. He urged them all to eat. With dawn about to break, Paul called everyone together and proposed breakfast: "This is the fourteenth day we've gone without food. None of us has felt like eating! But I urge you to eat something now. You'll need strength for the rescue ahead. You're going to come out of this without even a scratch!" (Acts 27:33–34 MSG). After Paul said this, he took some bread and gave thanks to God in front of them all. Then he broke it and began to eat. Two hundred seventy-six shipmates were encouraged and ate some food themselves.

Conjure up in your mind this picture: Paul is facing a shipwreck with a bunch of guys who likely had never been to any church or synagogue in their lives. Yet he establishes credibility. He asks them to eat so they can gain strength to survive. But first he does something that's universally Christian: he takes bread, and then he gives thanks for it, then breaks it and begins to eat.

Instead of cowering in the corner, Paul observed communion of sorts, on the deck of a ship that was thought to be without hope. Not only was Paul a carrier

> The winds do blow. Storms do come. During those times, you have no control over what is happening, but God does.

of hope, but his example of trust also washed away much of the tone of fear that had defined the journey.

Paul wrote later, "Give thanks in all circumstances" (1 Thessalonians 5:18 NIV). When we trust, fear begins to slip out of the picture. Paul cuts right to the heart of the matter: "The Spirit helps us in our weakness" (Romans 8:26 NIV).

Sometimes words cannot express the fear we feel. Paul is saying that the Holy Spirit shares in the struggle.

Paul wrote that Christ meant more to him than anything in the world. As we look at how we deal with our fears, let's remember most of us will never have a list like Paul's. Five times he was given the traditional forty lashes because he wouldn't quit preaching. Three times he was beaten with rods; once he was stoned. Three times he was shipwrecked. He was left for dead outside of Lystra. On the road, he was often hungry, thirsty, and often without shelter. Paul conquered fear!

Many of our greatest fears have to do with change. When Paul writes, he is perhaps the most authentic human voice to address the weakness of all the different approaches we use to handle our fear. What Paul wants us to do is to *change from the inside out*. Paul wrote to the Ephesian Christians, "I pray … that you will be strengthened in your inner being" (Ephesians 3:16). He understood that the real enemies of life live within us.

Paul knew the answer to our fears. The more the Lord is our partner, the more He begins to change us within where we most need it. Fear begins to be replaced by faith, by trust.

Many of us become chained, prisoners of our fears. Paul knew something about being a prisoner. The apostle wrote from a prison in Rome to the church at Philippi. Imagine that if pen and paper had been available, Paul would have sketched out these words to help give him inner strength he so desperately needed.

This would be the headline: "For me, nothing is as wonderful as knowing Christ Jesus my Lord." One can almost imagine Paul recounting the reasons for his peace:

- **Because Christ** goes before me, preparing my way.
- **Because Christ** is beside me, companion of my days.
- **Because Christ** is beneath me, catching me when I fall.
- **Because Christ** is behind me, nurturing what I have left undone.
- **Because Christ** is within me ... coaching, leading, prompting.
- **Because Christ** is above me, loving me now and forever more.

Paul is not giving a testimony of prosperity from a chapel with cushioned pews and stained-glass windows. He is in prison, likely an old well hole, when he writes these words.

What do we do with our fears?

Think of the "do nots" children are given by their parents. *"Be careful when you cross the street." "Look both ways." "Don't talk to strangers."* By instilling these fears, they lay the foundation of trust. Eric Erickson of Harvard University wrote many decades ago that the most important gift a parent can give a child is trust.

> *One of the most important gifts God wants to give is the gift of trust.*

Trust is not an automatic component of our internal GPS, so trusting is a learned behavior requiring lifelong practice. Times of struggle are never going to be fully understood. Learning to trust the One who gives us strength for the journey is crucial until we begin to see how it all fits together. Things are not often completed independently. God and others are needed to reach the finish.

Unlike any other life stage, fear in one's later years is often based on things that very well may happen. *Of all the topics on which I've lectured, none has resonated with listeners as much as this one: overcoming fear.* When I spoke about this topic recently, my later-life audience wanted my notes. They really needed to see two things: 1) that these fears were real; and 2) that they weren't alone. All I did in my lecture was to list the top ten fears identified by those in later life and by their caregivers. That was all I needed to say. The response from retirement center residents was instantaneous and powerful. I had struck a nerve. That means something significant: *You are not alone in your fears![1]* These were the top ten fears:

1. Declining health
2. Running out of money
3. Not being able to live at home or choose where to live
4. Death of a spouse or other close family member
5. Inability to manage daily activities
6. Not being able to drive
7. Isolation or loneliness

8. Strangers as caregivers
9. Fear of falling or hurting oneself
10. Loss of independence

Perhaps part of what participants needed was something we all need to do: *name* our fears. Once named, then the tough questions can be addressed head on: How will we respond to this fear? Some handle their fears by ignoring them or running away from them. But that strategy simply won't work.

Emilie Griffin, writer and founding member of Chrysostom Society, the national group for writers of faith, was fifty-six years old when she saw a shift in herself; that shift occurred when her mother's own aging seemed to abruptly appear in a day. Suddenly, she writes in her book, *Souls in Full Sail*, "it seemed I was in charge and had to move into high gear to take responsibility for her." In time, Griffin "came to write about the later years, my mother's and my own. ... I wanted to voice my fears about change and also the strengthening power of spiritual life."[2] She came to realize that "everyone is afraid of vulnerability, of falling. Losing one's dignity is only half of it. No one wants to lose control ... We want to relive and recapture the times when we were at the center of things."[3] We all long to be free, to maintain our personal independence. "I have my own yearnings for freedom," Griffin writes, "I want to be footloose and free." But, she concludes, "freedom comes as a realization that we are loved, accepted in the deepest sense, secure." Yes, "intimate friendship with God sets us free." In the end, "what we need most is spiritual courage. We need a biblical imagination to see God as he really is, in all his tenderness and power."[4]

So, if going around our fears is not an option, the only way out is through. To continue the journey, repacking our responses may shed light on the fact that there is one thing we can control: our response.

—Repacking Our Responses—

Our responses in any situation can define us. With fear, repacking is a process that must come from the inside out, since this is fear's home and hearth. After repacking our responses, our suitcase will be free for the journey.

Apostle Paul wrote to his son in faith: "God did not give us a spirit of cowardice, but rather a spirit of power and love and a sound mind" (2 Timothy 1:7).

The kind of love that's needed, Paul says, comes from the One "who has begun a good work in you." In other words, the Lord realizes trust is a journey, and He will be with us. His

> "I am convinced that life is 10 percent what happens to me and 90 percent how I react to it."
> —Charles Swindoll

love is the underpinning that enables us to move toward trust.

In *Waiting for God*, the French-born philosopher and author, Simone Weil, states that most people forget that the tree is as deeply rooted in the sun as it is rooted in the earth; therefore we are as deeply rooted in God more than we are in anything on earth. These deep roots are our personal relationship with the Lord.[5]

—The Jolts along Life's Journey—

There are times where the Lord is our best resource. In our earlier years, we attempted a lot of solo missions. Hopefully, we've learned that our own strength, will, and independence (or another's) will just not cut it. We might find ourselves being like a young boy who made a mess on the kitchen floor. His mother told him to get the broom off the back porch and clean it up. He told her it was dark out on the porch and he was afraid. She responded to him to not to be afraid because Jesus was there and would take care of him. The little boy opened the back door just a bit, stood on the threshold peering into the darkness, and said, "Jesus, will you please hand me the broom?"

That's what the Apostle would call the *natural* us. We stand looking at the back porch of the future, frozen, asking, "Jesus, will you please hand me the broom?"

As a nation, we have felt this over the years—Pearl Harbor, Oklahoma City, 9/11, just to name a few. Personally, we experience these same jolting experiences, which cause us to do "the inward-outward grief walk." Outside we're functioning somewhat normally. We have our "get-it-done faces" on, because it's expected. Inside it's a different picture. There's an open wound of loss. Fear has

> *"Being confident of this, that he who began a good work in you will carry it on to completion until the day of Christ Jesus."*
> —Philippians 1:6 NIV

taken up residence and thinks it has squatter's rights. Paul knew this struggle and wrote to his younger friend, Timothy, words to help him, and us, deal with the invasion of fear.

—Coward in the Corner—

Paul begins with a contrast: cowardice vs. courage. He stated that *cowardice is not part of God's will for our lives.* The word Paul uses for *cowardice* is a Greek word found only once in the New Testament—only here. *Courage*, on the other hand, along with the words *faith* and *trust* are found frequently in the New Testament. And for good reason. The devil holds the deed to cowardice. Our Lord Jesus holds the deed to trust that overcomes fear.

There's a great difference between being fearful and being a coward. There's a difference between the questions "Are you fearful?" and "Are you a coward?" Fear is admitted, while cowardice is not part of our resume. We admit we often fear. We can replace this fear with trust. When fear comes into our mind, it needs to be given its walking papers. It is faith and trust that wave fear good-bye.

What is the difference between being fearful and being a coward? The difference is immense, and Paul likely knew it since "sound mind" was part of the trinity of resources the Holy Spirit gives us. He'd encourage us to use our minds to navigate our responses to fear. Paul's final group of words in that scripture means "a carefully focused and regulated life." In the language of the New Testament, it's a single word, but it's difficult to translate into English with just one word. It can be translated as a "sound mind," "self-discipline," or "good sense," among other phrases. In *The Message: The Bible in Contemporary Language*, Eugene H. Peterson offers a useful translation for this word: "sensible." Paul might tell us to focus our attention to what God is doing in His world and in our lives.

—*Fear*—

Fear, like any emotion, can be consuming. It may take your breath away. Drowning in it keeps you from embracing any other deep emotion: joy, contentment, etc. It also prevents you from seeing God's plan and purpose for each day.

This kind of consuming fear often comes from an intimate situation. For me, it was the fear of Alzheimer's, since there are indelible images in my mind of my mother's difficult journey.

It's our personal fears that the Lord especially needs to carry for us. We aren't designed to do that kind of heavy lifting.

To Ignore Fear

One response to fear is to ignore it, to pretend it isn't there, to hope it will go away. But this ultimately leads to either anger or depression. Ignoring fear exacts a high price. If our fear turns into anger, we take it out on other people. If our fear turns into depression, we've let fear win the battle.

To Run Away From Fear

The second thing we can do with our fear is run away from it. This is the way of cowardice, of timidity, of being like the little boy, frozen at the door of the back porch, asking Jesus to do something we're supposed to do for ourselves.

To *Lean Into* Fear

But there's a better way to use our minds to move into our fear. We can, with God's strength and courage, lean into it with trust. The first step to overcoming fear is from right where you are. The Lord will walk you through it. He will walk *with* you, but He won't make the walk *for* you. This is something you two must do together.

Fear's good friend is guilt. This is what we feel when we fall short. Then we become our own worst critic. Resist that role. Better instead to admit our vulnerability and fully embrace the help of our Lord. If we were all perfect, there would have been no need for the cross. If we all made the perfect response to everything, there would have been no need for Christ. The Christian answer is not to always get everything right the first time. The Christian response of salvation is to redeem the situation by our second response.

When trust is in place, leaning into our fears can happen. Our minds have to release the grip of tough experiences or memories. Being born during the Great

> *If we were all perfect, there would have been no need for the cross. The Lord will help us face our fears.*

Depression was a defining experience for many. Parents may not have had jobs. There was seldom enough to eat. These are indelible memories: Dust Bowl days, when the wind would catch the farmland and turn it into huge black clouds rolling over the horizon like night in the middle of the day. This Great Depression produced many children who were born in a time of fear. But fear is a poor place to live.

Trust also requires looking at our own desires. Dr. Andrew Selle of Vermont Christian Counseling and Meditation Ministry writes about one woman he is helping. "Joan is afraid of dying; she wants to live … She is afraid of looking foolish; she wants others to see her as wise and spiritually mature. She fears her husband's rejection; she desires his acceptance and love." Fear and desire entwined.[6]

Interestingly enough, what we need here is trust—trust in the Lord. To trust Him is a total acknowledgement of all God is. This comes through knowing Him and His attributes, the greatest of which is His love for us. His love for us is what compels us to trust Him.

> "Our desires can eclipse our love for God."
> —Dr. Andrew Selle

Even if we lean into fear in later life, there will be some pretty powerful storms. Trusting God can feel like sailing in unchartered water. As we reflect back on our lives, our fears pale in comparison to Paul's experiences.

Ruth Graham, daughter of Billy Graham, focused her book, *A Legacy of Faith*, on the legacy that she has through her father. Ruth shared a terribly difficult time in her younger years when she was away at school and her father wrote to her: "There are two little words that I have used time after time when I have faced problems, dilemmas, and even the devil. They are: 'Fear not.'"

Someone has called these two words the *divine hush* for God's children, and Billy Graham continues his letter to Ruth, his daughter: "All of us face problems in our lives when we need the divine hush."

Thus Billy continues (with great affection, as he refers to Ruth by her nickname, Bunny):

> Now the devil is going to try to get you down a thousand times. He is going to work every angle. He is an old and

experienced hand at discouragement, and especially at trying to sidetrack young people. But ... Remember, dear Bunny, we love you, but God loves you even more! Even while you are sleeping He is at work with your problems.[7]

CHAPTER 5

The Anna Discovery:
Unexpected Joy Late in Life

*Trust in the Lord with all your heart, and
do not lean on your own understanding.
In all your ways acknowledge him and
he will make your paths straight.*
—Proverbs 3:5–6 NAS

The Anna Discovery

Unexpected Joy Late in Life

—Are We Out of Sync with God?—

One of the fascinating things about God is how He chooses the unlikely ones to weave His will among humankind. For example, who would have thought God would choose an eighty-year-old shepherd named Moses to liberate His people from bondage and lead them to the Promised Land? And who would have expected that Saul of Tarsus, archenemy of the church, would be chosen to become an apostle and the author of thirteen of the twenty-seven books in the Bible's New Testament?

But nothing can compare to the surprise of how God announced the arrival of His son and our savior, Jesus. God brings out a choir of angels, but whom does He choose to be the audience? Kings? Pharisees? Clergymen? Priests? No ... shepherds! And where is Jesus born? In a castle? A first-century hospital of sorts? No ... a lowly animal stable! And to whom will He choose to report what's happening and what God is doing?

Some first-century reporter? A representative from the king's palace? A Roman ambassador representing Caesar?

No! God chooses two eighty-year-olds who had regular prayer patterns at the temple: Anna and Simeon. The Bible only mentions Anna and Simeon in the

> *Our culture encourages us to fight the aging process through the promotion of products, services, and procedures.*

context of Christ's birth, but they're in sync with what God is doing, and God is in sync with their unique needs. *Obviously, God has a special place on the divine horizon for us, no matter what our age.*

In our current culture, age is often portrayed as a liability. We're expected to stay *young*, to think *young*, to look *young*. In 2009, we spent approximately $72 billion on anti-aging products and services. The mainstream message is insistent: If we want to stay young we must take steps to reverse the aging process itself: cosmetics, plastic surgery, etc. Less drastically, we are encouraged to keep buying the things we bought when we were younger.

I'm reminded of a story I heard about a young volunteer at a hospital. When she saw an older woman coming down the hall using a walker, she held the elevator for her. The older woman was moving quite slowly. When she finally reached the elevator, the older woman started to apologize, but the young volunteer waved it away: "I know the walker must be tough to manage," she said.

The older woman turned to her and said, "No, the walker's not a problem, but I've just bought these new shoes and they're killing my feet!" I expect many of us living through later life have been in those shoes.

Our culture encourages people to fight the aging process. What we seem unable to embrace is that there are advantages to growing older. With age comes wisdom, clarity, perspective, and experience. *But the greatest advantage to growing older is having the opportunity to access your spiritual self, to see its possibilities and nurture its strengthening power.* The spiritual self doesn't grow old. In many older people, it becomes *more vibrant.*

—*Anna and Simeon*—

To emphasize the possibilities of the power of our later years, look at two unlikely people who celebrated with Joseph and Mary the birth of Jesus: Anna and Simeon. (Follow the story of their meeting the baby Jesus in the Temple at Jerusalem in Luke 2:21–39.)

In the birth of Jesus, we see God's low-key, simple,

> *Anna "was of a great age"– eighty-four years old, and a widow for more than sixty years.*
>
> —Luke 2:36-37

understated way of announcing the Savior. Anna and Simeon had grown into keen spiritual awareness. Each had a very different journey, which brought them to the temple.

—*Anna: The Nurturer*—

Life was not easy for Anna. Losing her husband when she was very young, Anna spent more than sixty years as a widow in a male-

> *Anna was a remarkable woman, particularly given the time in which she lived.*

dominated world. She could have easily gone through life asking, "Why me?" and disappear in despair. She would never have been missed. By the world's standard, Anna had done nothing significant in her younger years. Besides, in her day, the list was short—bear a child. As a woman, she surely wouldn't be offered a position in the temple. Nonetheless, Anna rooted herself at the temple, fasting, praying, and expecting great things from God.

People who visited the temple respected her; she was always there! The Scripture calls her a prophet. First, Simeon told Mary and Joseph that their baby was the Messiah. Then Anna saw baby Jesus, and she too prophesized that He was Israel's long-awaited redeemer. Those gathered at the temple that day paid attention to what Anna had to say. That they respected the words of this poor widow woman was remarkable in itself, given the male-dominated time in which Anna lived.

Ironically, even though she didn't nurture a child, Anna had something in full measure, which all women seem to have to some degree: she was a nurturer. From the earliest of times, women have been seen as caregivers. To nurture involves feeding, encouraging, and protecting. From rearing children, to helping with siblings, to looking after companies and employees, most women throughout their lives experience the joys and heartbreak of being a nurturer.

—*Nurturing Yourself*—

In later life, we have both the time and motivation to nurture the spiritual side of ourselves. You may still be a nurturer for others, but you have the primary gift of time and even preoccupation of growing a spiritually sensitive self.

Anna made the conscious choice to nurture her relationship with God during her long widowhood. She could have given into despair and become a bitter woman, but as she began to recover from her grief, she remained expectant that God would reveal Himself if she was steadfast.

> *The Lord is good to those who wait for him, to the soul who seeks him.* (Lamentations 3:25 ESV)

Scripture tells us she spent a great deal of time in prayer. Sociologists Susan Melia and Susan McFadden have documented that Anna was on to something. In their study, they discovered that prayer has a very significant role in the lives of many older women. They studied and interviewed women ages sixty-five to ninety-eight, both Catholic and Protestant. Consistently the women they studied and interviewed embraced "prayer as a constant activity." It's a "fuel," *a way of connecting*, and many times, *a way of coping*. They described prayer as a relationship with God, an opportunity to be in God's presence, and a possible means of allowing God to speak through them.[1]

One participant stated, "I don't just think of prayer as a bowing of the head and folding of the hands. I think of it as more of an attitude toward life and toward people. It is kind of like practicing the presence of God. Things go better for me when I can be conscious of that spirit as I do whatever I do."

The women also reported they have more time and space for prayer than younger women. Many use prayer to give structure to their days. One Catholic sister commented that even though she couldn't read anymore, "I love to pray. Each day I say the rosary—three complete beads. I say one for our sisters who are working, one for all my pupils who are still alive, and one for the sisters who are sick."

Melia and McFadden reported that the way women of later years pray is likely to change in several ways. It has become "more simple, spontaneous, intimate, meaningful, personal, flexible and open with God as a valued companion." In essence, these who are by nature nurturers have learned to nurture their relationship with God.

Perhaps this can be summed up by a participant who stated, "I've experienced an increase in my spiritual appetite."

The study reported that prayer is:

- A source of connection with others, an opportunity to continue nurturing those relationships and especially their relationship with God;
- A means to reduce their sense of loneliness and enhance their sense of gratitude;
- A way to structure their days into comfortable routines, and lead them to accept their lives and to foster forgiveness;
- A form of contributing to those around them, and believing that the words, thoughts and meditations of their hearts contribute to the healing of the world.

—Nurturing in Our Later Years—

British researchers have been following centenarians for some years now and have studied what makes them vital and engaged at over one hundred years old. One of the common themes is spirituality. These centenarians are profound believers in the spiritual and are actively engaged in it. They may not be officially aligned with a religious group, may not be able to attend religious services, but their inner lives are alive with the Spirit.[2]

The Apostle Paul discovered the same thing. In his later years, writing to the Corinthian Christians, he stated:

> So we do not lose heart. Even though our outer nature is wasting away, our inner nature is being renewed day by day. For this slight momentary affliction is preparing us for an eternal weight of glory beyond all measure, because we look not at what can be seen but at what cannot be seen; for what can be seen is temporary, but what cannot be seen is eternal. (2 Corinthians 4:16–18)

Nurturing one's own self is a spiritual need. Anna had learned that during her long and often difficult life, and her discovery can be a powerful lesson for us as well. But the essential point is that Anna did not merely nurture the part of herself seen by others. She also nurtured "what cannot be seen." She understood what Paul would come to understand in his own later life: *what can be seen is temporary, but what cannot be seen is eternal.*

CHAPTER 6

The Esther Discovery:
The Quiet Presence of Courage

Do not fear, for I am with you,
do not be afraid, for I am your God;
I will strengthen you, I will help you,
I will uphold you with my victorious right hand.
—Isaiah 41:10

The Esther Discovery

The Quiet Presence of Courage

—*Transforming Minuses to Pluses*—

In his book *The Art of Passing Over*, Francis Dorff states that in the bias of our culture, we have a tendency to grade our lives in three ways. We give youth a decided "plus," middle age a perplexed "plus-minus with a question mark," and our older years "a definite minus, if we considered it rating-worthy at all."[1]

Each life stage has its shares of pluses and minuses. The same is true for each generation, so one shouldn't be surprised to discover the same is true for those in biblical times. We might miss it in the Old Testament book of Esther, because true to our culture, we take a story and glamorize it, clean it up, or broadcast it at such a level that the real story's nearly lost. Over the years, the story of Esther has been portrayed like any other princess story with a fairy-tale happy ending, focusing little on the tragic chapters of her early life.

A Jew living in the country of Persia, Esther's family tree traced her back to the tribe of Benjamin, also known as Hadassah, which

> *Esther's early life wasn't peaceful or one that would evoke a spirit of gratitude.*

means "Myrtle," a name in the ancient world that symbolized peace and thanksgiving. The truth is, Esther's early life wasn't peaceful, stable, or normal, or one that would evoke a spirit of gratitude. Her parents both died while she was very young, and her older cousin, Mordecai, was the only one available to take her in. So, if you asked Esther to rate her pluses and minuses at that point, she could've handily played the minus card and journeyed many miles down a negative path. Furthermore, Esther and Mordecai lived during a very difficult time. They were forced to live in a foreign country with no future to call their own.

—True Beauty Within —

Mordecai did the best he could for this child orphan. He stepped up to raise her and helped her many times along her journey.

Xerxes I, of the Persian Empire (known in the book of Esther as King Ahasuerus), was a rich and extravagant king. He was so wrapped up in his power and pride that he decided to put his wealth on display for six months, culminating with a seven-day feast. On the last day of the feast, King Xerxes called for Queen Vashti to display her beauty to the people. She refused and was banished from the king's presence for the rest of her life. Harsh punishment? She was lucky he didn't kill her for refusing him. At this time in history, a woman, even a queen, couldn't risk contributing her own opinion. So, Xerxes began the search for a new queen. He ordered officials throughout Persia to send the most beautiful women in the kingdom from which he could choose a new queen.

Esther was chosen as a candidate and eventually as Xerxes' new queen. In accordance with Mordecai's counsel, she did not reveal that she was a Jew—one of

> *Esther showed a faith that ignored boundaries and sought instead open and willing hearts.*

the many thousands scattered throughout Persia after their exile from Jerusalem. Despite her newfound luxury and status, she maintained her faith in the God of Israel—which her new and touchy King of course did not. According to the version of the Book of Esther found in the Eastern Orthodox Church (and in the book called "Esther (Greek)" or "Additions to Esther" in the Apocrypha of other Christian versions of the Bible), Esther was actually miserable as queen. On official occasions, she dressed and acted the part. In private, she dressed in traditional Jewish garb and maintained the religious traditions of her Hebrew God. She felt her role as Queen was a vulgar and pagan sin against her God. But she trusted Mordecai's advice—and well she did.

While she was Queen of Persia, a power-hungry man named Haman took offense at Mordecai and his faith; he hatched a plan to kill all the Jews in Xerxes' kingdom. In the end, however, the courage and wisdom of Mordecai and Esther thwarted Haman's plan. They not only prevented this genocide but also won revenge against Haman and his allies. This turning of the tables then formed the basis of the traditional Hebrew festival of Purim. What was more, Xerxes came to believe in Esther's God.

For our purposes, however, we need to look more closely at Esther's behavior as the possibility of genocide unfolded. In the Orthodox version, she is advised by Mordecai to reveal her faith to Xerxes and to use her influence with the king to stop the massacre of Jews. What influence? The king had exiled his previous queen for not coming when he called for her. What would he do to his new queen when she asked him to change his decree because she herself was Jewish? But she knew Mordecai was right, and she had both the courage and faith to act.

First, she acted to make things right in her own heart, rejecting her outward beauty for her inward beauty. She "took off her splendid apparel and put on the garments of distress and mourning, and instead of costly perfumes she covered her head with ashes and dung" [Esther (Greek) 14: 1-2 ESV]. Then, she prayed for courage in confronting the king, for protection of the people of Israel. Finally, she confessed to God her deepest feelings of discontent as a Jewish queen in a pagan kingdom. "You know my necessity," she prayed, "that I abhor the sign of my proud position . . . I abhor it like a menstrual rag. . . . Your servant has had no joy since the day that I was brought here until now, except in you, O Lord God of Abraham" [Esther (Greek) 14: 16-19 ESV].

Strong words. Painful words. But from that prayer she found a strong foundation upon which she dared to change the king's mind. She confronted Xerxes with fear and trembling, knowing he might kill her. But she did it. And she succeeded in changing his mind—and the law! Esther's inner beauty and courage saved the Jews of ancient Persia and spread the acceptance of the God of Abraham.

Esther showed a trusting heart and mind, and she grew to see that God is present even when He seems nowhere. She remained committed to family and faith amidst desperate uncertainty.

—Just As I Am—

The story of Esther teaches an important lesson for those of us confronting the uncertainties and struggles of later life. It reminds us that faith in God and His presence is more than a simple belief or wish. For Esther, *faith was manifested in action.* God gave her important gifts—a wise and loving cousin, a natural beauty, an innate good sense of how to overcome difficult situations. But to save her people, Esther had to take action. She had to take very risky action.

Where did she find her courage? She never lost sight of who she was. As a queen of a rich and massive kingdom, she might well have turned her back on her past. She did not. One senses in her prayer to God an understanding that to lose her past and her faith was to lose her self, to lose the meaning of her own life. She came to realize, in her moment of crisis, that God could use her just as she was. Only as her true self—a faithful Jew who had come through hard times to become Queen of Persia—could she be in a position to be of service to others.

Think about the pluses and minuses of Esther's life. She did not dwell on things most of us would put in the minus column. Instead, she embraced the positives of her upbringing: being brought up by a wise and faithful cousin in a close-knit community of Jewish exiles. Later, even as Queen of Persia, she did not consider all of the external pluses as glorious positives. Through all of her ups and downs, Esther kept sight of who she really was. Through Mordecai's teachings and her own watchful evaluation of her position as queen, she understood that God loved her just as she was. God had a job for her, a job *just for her*. But, like Abraham, she had to say yes. She had to take a leap of faith.

—*Risking It All*—

When Haman hatched his plot to kill all of the Jews in the kingdom, it seemed there was no one who could stop him. He had issued the order with the king's official seal. The order had to be carried out. The only way would be to convince Xerxes to rescind his own decree. No one was in a position to do that. Well, almost no one.

> *Like Esther and Mordecai, "everyone who belongs to God may be proficient, equipped for every good work."*
> —2 Timothy 3:17

Mordecai came to Esther and pled for her to intercede to the king. But this brought out the real problem. The king didn't know Esther was a Jew, and she had no idea how he would respond to the news. She faced the real possibility of losing not only her position as queen but of being executed for being a Jewess. The previous queen had been banished for less.

> *"For if you keep silence at such a time as this, relief and deliverance will rise for the Jews from another quarter, but you and your father's family will perish. Who knows? Perhaps you have come to royal dignity for just such a time as this."*
> —Esther 4:14

Initially, Esther was reluctant. But Mordecai persisted, and his words to Esther remain some of the most memorable lines in the story of Esther. "Who knows?" he asks, "Perhaps you have come to royal dignity for just such a time as this" (Esther 4:14). She prayed about it. She asked the Jews of the kingdom to fast and pray. She made her choice. Through faith, she took action.

Look at a graph below. It illustrates the story of Esther, event by event. Become aware of the small steps God used to bring about His purpose.

Esther is adopted by her older cousin Mordecai
King Xerxes throws a lavish party
Queen Vashti refuses the king's command and is removed from the throne.
King Xerxes chooses Esther as his new queen
Mordecai uncovers a plot to assassinate the king and informs Esther, who in turn informs the king
King Xerxes' officiant, Haman, devises a plan to kill the Jews because Mordecai refuses to bow down before Haman
Mordecai learns of the plan and tells Esther; she urges the Jews to pray and fast
Esther informs the king and confronts Haman
King Xerxes sides with Esther and orders the death of Haman

Many times God doesn't show Himself in a way obvious to us, and yet we can be sure that He is silently and continually at work in our lives to accomplish His good purposes.

Despite her fears, Esther put her life on the line with an appeal to King Xerxes. For the first time there was an outward expression of her faith when she asked Mordecai to organize a time of fasting. Esther knew this practice wasn't about food, but was a godly exercise, which would bring the Jewish community closer to God. The orphan girl turned queen recognized the huge "plus" in her position, as well as how that position could be put to life-saving purpose, but she had to risk her very life to save her people.

When Esther met with the king, all went well, for the king responded graciously and granted Esther's request. The Jewish people were spared. Haman was justly destroyed, being hanged on the same gallows he had prepared for Mordecai.

Imagine Esther's heart and swell of emotions. Devastated and frightened, she had acted courageously. In so doing, she remained focused by drawing upon Mordecai's training and her well-honed understanding of how the royal court operated. She asked God for help. She instructed the Jews of the kingdom to fast, to do their part. She planned and acted in the way best suited to success. The king listened and proved wise. The Jewish nation, through which Christ would come, was preserved. Esther's heart must have nearly burst with joy.

Esther must have had a sense of the providence, preservation, and care God exercises over all creation. God's providence doesn't often employ awe-inspiring miracles. Instead, He often uses the natural laws of our world—and our very common selves—to accomplish His will.

Providence is also very complex for us because our human perspective limits us. The intricate weavings of God's workings in history are sometimes better appreciated than investigated. Look at the graph again and think about God's complicated ways. There is a great practical lesson here for us: Keep believing. God does indeed work in mysterious ways.

But suppose Esther never took a chance, never stepped out in courage, never left her comfort zone and moved into God's arms? She would have lived with regrets the rest of her life. It's a question we must ask ourselves. Risks or regrets?

A recent survey by Bronnie Ware, a nurse from Australia, studied regret in later life. Ware listened to the regrets of those on their deathbed, and the results have direct meaning for us.[2] These were the top five regrets:

1. I wish I would have had the courage to live a life true to myself, not the life others expected of me.
2. I wish I had not worked so hard (especially common among males).
3. I wish I would have had the courage to express my feelings.
4. I wish I had stayed in touch with my friends.
5. I wish I had let myself be happier.

Ouch. Some of these hit a little too close to home. All of us in our later lives have heard someone voicing such regrets. We have voiced them ourselves.

Why? Why would we live our lives in ways that left us with feelings of regret? Why would we not embrace our true selves, take a little extra time for friends and family, express our true feelings more freely, and allow ourselves to stop and smell the roses along the way? The answer, in part, is that there is always a risk to being fully you.

Consider Esther's grueling decision. None of her options looked promising. Option #1: She could risk her own life, be executed, and still fail to stop the mass murder of her people. Option #2: She could keep silent about the Jews and maintain her life and her high position in the Persian kingdom, but then she would live with lifelong regret about keeping silent; indeed, she would live with blood on her hands. Option #3: She could be her true self and try her best, given her situation, and maybe, with God's help, she could succeed. Call it a miracle. Call it God's plan. But recognize that God worked through Esther. She had to say yes to God. She had to take a leap of faith, and that is what she did. She chose to get right with God, to reveal her true self, and to use her God-given gifts to save her people.

Risks or regrets? Almost everyone in later life has regrets, of course. But our lives are not over! We still have time to say yes to God and to allow Him to work through us. Esther chose wisely and courageously. Let us do the same. If we do, we will discover unique pluses in our final years.

—*The Pluses of Later Life*—

Any stage in life has pluses and minuses. Think about the many transitions you made in earlier years: schools, jobs, marriage, parenthood, moving from one place to another. Always, there were challenges. It may be that we are better equipped to confront challenges later in life. Consider some recent research—and its surprising and heartening results!

Elliott Dorff, author of *The Matters of Life and Death*, gives us a practical look at pluses and minuses. The cultural assessment of where we are in our lifespan is often to draw a circle around our later years and write "minus" above it. Can we accept the negatives as part of our reality while still embracing the significant positives woven into life's remaining years?[3]

If we open ourselves up to the pluses, we can place ourselves in the positive camp in our later years. If we shift our focus, try to release what holds us back from a full season of life, then we may indeed sense the presence and plan of the One who's brought us this far along the way. Later life has its advantages.

Consumer Reports, in a 2013 report on aging, listed the *five good things about aging:*[4]

1. *Anger, stress, and worry are less common*

A 2010 Gallup survey, published in the *Proceedings of the National Academy of Sciences,* surveyed more than 340,000 Americans and drew comparisons of stress, worry, and anger in the earlier years as compared to the later years. Summarizing the data, Dr. Laura Carstensen, PhD of Stanford University, was quoted as saying, "As people get older, they're more likely to stop and smell the roses. We think that has a lot do with these improvements that we see in emotional health."

2. *Wisdom Grows*

Researchers at the University of Michigan and the University of Texas in Dallas studied people between the ages of twenty-five and ninety-three. Significantly, more older people ranked in the top 20 percent on wisdom performance. Apparently the brain clings to its experience-based knowledge well into old age.

3. *Marriages get healthier*

Married seniors report greater satisfaction and more positive experiences with their mates than younger married couples, even when they quarrel. Marital harmony in old age is especially important because senior couples tend to enjoy better health and quality of life than their unmarried peers.

4. Satisfaction with social relationships grows

Seniors typically have a smaller but closer circle of friends than younger adults, research shows. Older people tend to focus on close friends and family members who are important in meeting their emotional needs.

5. Happiness increases

Feelings of emotional well-being may not only improve your quality of life but also add years to it. Researchers at Stanford University followed the emotional health of 184 adults ages 18 to 94 for 10 years. Those who experienced more positive than negative emotions in everyday life were more likely to have survived over a longer period, according to the March 2011 report in *Psychology and Aging*.

So, like Esther, we must list out our pluses—some of which we may be able to draw out of the earlier list. If we're not careful, we could be preoccupied with our minuses. Or, like Esther, we could wait and watch to see what God will do through each of them. In our watching and waiting, we can be reminded that *even in times when He seems nowhere about, God is very much with us, preparing us, partnering with us, each step of the way.*

CHAPTER 7

The Joseph Discovery:
Embracing New Normals

It is the Lord who goes before you. He will be with you; he will not leave you or forsake you. Do not fear or be dismayed.
—Deuteronomy 31:8 ESV

The Joseph Discovery

Embracing New Normals

In recent years, our culture has merged *new* and *normal* into *new normal*. The NBC television network embraced it in the title of a sitcom, showcasing that life does present many new normals, no matter what your age or stage of life. A new normal can be abrupt, unexpected. Even if it's expected, what lies ahead is often unclear. If something is new, it isn't normal. If something is normal, it isn't new. But a truth about life is there are times when both words describe where we are or where we need to be.

If you think about it, putting new and normal together is not new at all. In life there are naturally occurring *new normal* times.

> *At first glance, new and normal would seem to contradict each other.*

- **Entering kindergarten or first grade, going to school was *new* but soon became *normal*;**
- **Leaving home to begin work, military service, college, or any other transition in life. It was *new* for a while**

but then became a *normal* situation, moving toward independence and adulthood;

- **Getting married;**
- **Becoming parents.**

There are other times in life that often demand radical adjustment to a *new normal* such as:

Divorce—This is a *new normal*
These are always times that we chart a course we never intended.

Health crisis—This is a *new normal*
Medical emergencies or new diagnoses may come, which we've not anticipated.

Professional crisis—This is a *new normal*
Change in one's job or profession, even the loss of employment.

Death—This is a *new normal*
The loss of a loved one, whether a spouse, partner, or family member, can be devastating and require new life strategies.

Retirement—This is a *new normal*
We may relinquish much of what has made us comfortable, successful—normal. But the future has intriguing possibilities.

Many of our *new normals* come in later life when we find ourselves in situations we didn't anticipate. A chaplain at a retirement center told me the story of Jenny. Her husband went into the hospital for a knee replacement. She had jitters, but, as the doctors reassured her, this kind of surgery was routine. But after the routine surgery, things took a turn for the worse. Then catastrophe. Jenny found herself planning a memorial service. Over the coming days, weeks, months, and even years, Jenny began to say she was finding her *new normal*. For her, the new normal emerged slowly. Grief and loss were the most difficult to live through. *Some new normals stretch us beyond that which we'd envisioned as our capabilities.*

So, how do we navigate a *new normal*? We can learn from the biblical character Joseph. He lived through more new normals than most of us can even imagine. He not only navigated the treacherous times he lived through, he ultimately came out on top. He's one whose story is a powerful instruction.

—*The Amazing Life of Joseph*—

One conservative Bible teacher describes Joseph as the person most like Jesus in all of the Old Testament.[1] Joseph's story is found in Genesis. He is someone worth looking at, and learning from, because he had to enter and live through

> *What does that boy with the rainbow-colored coat have to do with us? All of his life, Joseph was in one new normal after another, most of which were not of his own choosing.*

so many *new normals*. In the process he learned to come out on top. The question is, *how did he do it?*

—*Joseph's Story Begins*—

In ancient times, a male-dominated society, a man of position usually had several wives and many children, as did Joseph's father, Jacob. Having many sons afforded more hands to work the crops, tend the sheep, and work the cattle. More hands also meant a greater chance of conflict within the community of sons.

Jacob set the stage for the band of brothers to clearly see Joseph as the apple of Jacob's eye. Through outward expressions, Jacob

> *The coat of many colors became a symbol of Jacob's preference for Joseph.*

lavished his love on Joseph, giving him a very expensive and beautiful coat of many colors. The color of jealousy from his brothers was as intense as the jewel tones in the fabric of Joseph's coat.

One day Jacob sent Joseph out into the fields with food for his brothers. Joseph, the youngest, was the delivery boy. His brothers saw him coming wearing the coat they detested. They devised a demonic plot. They would get rid of Joseph, kill a lamb, and sprinkle his robe with the lamb's blood, and then report to their father that a wild beast had killed him.

Even as they were hatching their plot, another group appeared on the horizon: Ishmaelites from Midian. They frequently passed through on their way to Egypt, often with goods and slaves to sell in Egypt. Suddenly a new idea surfaced. *Let's sell Joseph to the Ishmaelites,* they reasoned. *We'll get a pocket full of money. We can still kill the lamb and take his bloody robe home as evidence that Jacob's beloved Joseph was killed by a wild animal.*

As unthinkable as it was, the brothers pulled it off, and Joseph was on his way to Egypt as a marketable young slave. What an unthinkable new normal! In one day, Joseph was changed from the favorite son of a wealthy landowner into a piece of human merchandise with a price tag on his brow. Joseph's early life was privileged and favored. Now everything had changed. The issue was whether he could recover and create his own new normal.

Joseph, now a slave, began a long and tedious journey to Egypt, perhaps on camels, perhaps on foot. And perhaps Joseph spent time on another journey, an *inward* journey. Joseph was a deeply perceptive person and turned into a person with spiritual possibilities. He doubtless tried to sort out what had happened to him. Was God in this? Did God live only in the land of Canaan? Or was there even a God?

Inwardly Joseph knew he had a choice. He could spend the rest of his life feeling bitter and betrayed. Or he could begin to believe God could help him work things out. The Apostle Paul wrote many centuries later: "We know that all things work together for good for those who love God" (Romans 8:28).

—*Inner Toughness*—

Eventually the Ishmaelites from Midian arrived in Egypt, and Joseph was part of their merchandise to be sold. After much negotiating, they sold Joseph to a wealthy man named Potiphar, a friend of the Egyptian king and chief of the king's guard. He was rich, had strategic contacts, and was a man of power. One thing Potiphar lacked was a son. Potiphar's wife became attracted to Joseph. Eventually he found out about her attraction, became furious, and Joseph wound up in the king's prison.

Joseph entered *another* new normal. Potiphar, who had treated Joseph as a favored son, now had him sent to prison. Life seemed determined to make a bitter man out of Joseph. But he had an *inner toughness*.

While in prison, Joseph made a friend, who later became one of the pharaoh's advisors. When the pharaoh had a dream he couldn't interpret, the friend remembered how Joseph had interpreted dreams correctly in the prison chamber. Joseph revealed there would be seven bountiful harvests, followed by seven years of drought and famine. Because of this revelation, the pharaoh put Joseph in charge of storing up grain during the bountiful years so there would be adequate food during the envisioned drought.

Joseph was able to oversee the harvests of the bounty years and store grain in anticipation of the famine that was to come. The famine did arrive. Joseph's planning and foresight allowed the Egyptians to not only survive, but to sell grain to the other nations.

Meanwhile, Joseph's family had *not* stored up grain for the years of famine. Jacob sent Joseph's brothers to Egypt in an attempt to purchase grain. The brothers had no idea that the Egyptian they were asking for food from was their brother. Without revealing who he was, Joseph arranged the transaction but with the stipulation that the brothers bring back their father. Joseph wished for a reunion.

Perhaps the most powerful statement Joseph makes in showing *forgiveness* is his family reunion. Unknowingly, the brothers

> *One of the great reunions of the Bible is between Joseph and his father and brothers.*

return and are before their brother. Joseph eventually reveals himself. This opens the door for him to reunite with his father, Jacob, and enable his family to survive.

What a reunion! Jacob realized his son, who he thought was dead, had survived in Egypt and was now in charge of distributing grain. It reminds us of the primacy that family relationships can play in moving to a *new normal*.

—*The Wound and the Scar*—

How did Joseph handle his life's circumstances? At some point, he must've been broken to his very core. His brothers sold him like property! How do we begin to accept a loss that seems permanent and learn to somehow get on with our lives? There is no simple formula; everyone's journey is different. But one way is to turn our wounds—our emotional and psychological wounds—into scars.

I was attending a memorial service for a fellow minister when his adopted son rose to speak. He related his father's lesson about turning wounds into scars.

The son recounted his early boyhood. He never knew his real father. When his mother died, his world seemed to come to an end.

The minister and his wife decided to adopt the boy when he was an early teen. But after the adoption, bitterness surfaced and lingered—a sour attitude toward everything and everyone.

One day when the bitterness of all that had been lost was particularly heavy, his adopted father called him into the woodshop where he was working. He said, "Son, the fact that you lost your mother was very tragic. I am sorry. But if you keep it as an open wound, as it is, it will likely kill you. But if you turn it into a scar, it will remain with you, but it will not *define or* destroy *you."*

Consider that a scar reflects something important that's happened, important enough to leave a personal, permanent mark. Though it remains, perhaps even visibly, it doesn't affect what's currently going on.

Then consider a wound. A wound is fresh, must be tended to every day, and affects the patterns of everyday life. Some wounds must be lived with, but most emotional wounds can eventually be turned into scars. They're remembered at special times, like anniversaries, but they do not have to affect the daily purposes of each day.

There is a choice for those who have suffered great loss, when it comes to the new normal in life. We can keep the wound fresh, whether it's the loss of a job, divorce, death of a loved one, or some other bitter

> *Turn the open wounds of painful memories into scars. The scar will never go away, but the wound will no longer remain open. And that will make all the difference.*

experience of the past. Or we can let the wound heal, leaving a scar, but a scar that allows us to get on with our lives.

Joseph was wise enough to know that before he could begin to deal with what was *ahead*, he had to deal with what was *behind*. He had to heal the wound of the betrayal by his brothers. *Joseph had to change the wound to a scar.*

—What Would You Have Done?—

Revenge? Some might spend the rest of their lives trying to get even. But a get-even mentality is like a cancer within the mind and heart, a deadly poison, which entraps, keeping us from fully moving ahead, missing tomorrow's full possibilities.

So the first necessity in learning to transform a wound to a scar is to deal with what has been. Remember the difference: a wound is always present tense. A scar is past tense. So *how do we transform a wound into a scar?*

—Forgiveness—

To change a wound into a scar the first step is often forgiveness. Somehow, somewhere along that great journey from Palestine to Egypt, Joseph had to handle the wrong that had been done to him. Decades later, when Joseph had become an Egyptian executive, the brothers who had sold him into slavery would come begging for food.

> *"My sorrows are mine and will not leave me. All I can do is give them to God, for in submitting them to God they take on meaning. When I do that I transform my heart to become a little more like that of Jesus."*
>
> —Henry Nouwen

The forgiveness Joseph granted in his heart earlier surfaced in the halls of Egyptian power.

Jesus taught that forgiveness from above is dependent upon forgiveness on earth: "For if you forgive others their trespasses, your heavenly Father will also forgive you" (Matthew 6:12 ESV). Joseph lived out that prayer a long time before Jesus prayed it.

—Characteristics of Joseph—

Joseph was great at rolling with the punches, mainly due to his internal strength.

He, like other centenarians (those who have lived to and beyond one hundred years of age), was able to keep going. It might be described as a good attitude, but it's also a certain self-toughness.

What are the characteristics of Joseph that may explain his ability to roll with each new misfortune that came his way?

Joseph had the ability to forge new relationships

One of the gifts or talents Joseph had in abundance was the ability to make friends. After being put in prison, he makes friends with two prison mates who have dreams they cannot figure out. They ask Joseph about them, and he interprets the dreams but loses the friends in the process.

The dream of the first friend indicates that he will be put to death, which happens as Joseph foretold: one friend was gone. The other friend's dream was in sharp contrast. Joseph interpreted his dream to mean he would be restored to his former position of status with the king. Once again, Joseph predicted the future correctly. The prisoner regained his elevated position in Egypt's royal hierarchy and seemingly forgot all about Joseph. Seemingly, Joseph had lost out again, but friendships made along the way have a way of coming back to bless us.

Joseph drew on his God-given ability

Not many people can relate to the gift of interpreting dreams, but we can all relate to some of Joseph's gifts, and hopefully to the fact that he used these abilities to navigate all situations—to survive, even thrive, in tough times.

Joseph was a born leader. He innately knew how to organize and make things happen. Because of his ability to get along with his fellow prisoners and lead them, eventually Joseph was put in charge of the other prisoners.

In our later years, key people with meaningful, needed relationships may *not* flow out of genetic bloodlines. Many of us have significant geographic boundaries from our families. Other boundaries and barriers exist as well—broken relationships, for example. For some of us, those we thought would outlive us did not. It may mean we redefine the term *family*. *Family* may become the person next door or a trusted friend. Some may have already discovered that close friends really do become family.

—What Can Joseph Teach Us About Our New Normal—

In our later years, we can anticipate certain situations, but we can't anticipate all that's on the horizon. Like Joseph, events beyond our control may overwhelm us. But, like him, we can change our own attitudes about our situation.

We have to imagine that Joseph must've spent a great deal of time remembering the past, all the moments when life went wrong and all seemed lost. But Joseph made it a habit to focus on ways he could improve the situation where ever God led him. Did he ever really forget the pain of being sold into slavery? Probably not. But he never allowed the injustices of the past to consume him. Instead, he continued to grow and to excel in places God could use him.

Remembering how you worked through difficult times in the past can help you navigate the present and the future. In doing so, you may need to:

1. Build a new system
2. Adapt an existing one
3. Look to the horizon, not the rearview mirror

And, you may need to release:

1. Your earlier independence (the "I got this" kind of attitude)
2. Earlier hurts that impede your journey
3. The expectations you held in early life

Paradoxically, looking to the past, in the rearview mirror so to speak, can give you a crucial glimpse of what lies ahead. Psychologists suggest our responses to life's challenges have a meaningful effect on how things turn out. It's not particularly scientific, but there's something to be said for facing a new normal with a "try, try again" spirit.

Psychologists, psychiatrists, counselors (and pastors) who research and spend a lot of time listening to people report that how people see themselves is crucial to how

> *The kinds of new normal we often face in our later years require celebrating small successes along the way.*

they handle their new normal. Do you see yourself as God sees you? Are we willing to let go of difficult times in the past and turn them from *wounds* to *scars*? Are we willing to forgive others? Are we willing to forge new relationships in whatever new normal we find ourselves? Will we call on our own inner toughness, not squelching our God-given gifts, but using them to navigate in our new normal?

CHAPTER 8

The Mary Discovery:

Healing a Broken Heart

Come to me, all you that are weary
and are carrying heavy burdens,
and I will give you rest.
Take my yoke upon you, and learn from me;
for I am gentle and humble in heart,
and you will find rest for your souls.
For my yoke is easy, and my burden is light.

—Matthew 11:28–30

The Mary Discovery

Healing a Broken Heart

—Growing Through Grief—

The Christmas season is a wonderful celebrative moment for Christians—the many-colored Christmas lights, a bright, fully decorated tree, and beautifully wrapped gifts. We celebrate the traditional Christmas story: Mary and Joseph in the stable with the baby Jesus surrounded by the shepherds and wise men.

Mary, the mother of Jesus, had received an incredible announcement, "Mary, you have been chosen to be the mother of the Messiah!"

Amidst her joy, she solemnly asks the obvious question, "How can this be?" (Luke 1:26–34). After all, she's a virgin, and, though engaged to Joseph, they have never been together as husband and wife. An angel of God tells her a miracle will happen ... and, it comes to pass. Jesus is born.

"How can this be?" will be a question woven throughout Mary's life. For her, joy and sorrow will almost always be comingled.

On the one hand, she's been given a priceless gift, and on the other hand, she'll know grief as few others have. Mary will live in that

> *Mary's struggle with loss will be the soil from which the flowers of faith will come.*

tender balance between the miracle of life and the struggle of grief and loss.

While the intensity of Mary's experience may be different from ours, the journey she walked may be similar. As we dwell on Mary's spiritual discoveries, we hear echoes of our own experiences. Mary's question—"How can this be?"—is a question that we, too, have asked as we have walked through the joys and sorrows of our own lives. It is a question asked by all of us living through later life—especially in moments of grief.

Nicholas Wolterstorff, author of *Lament for a Son*, writes about the "neverness" of grief. He experienced the dreadful loss of his son Eric when he fell to his death mountain climbing. Wolterstorff wrote:

> It is the *neverness* that is so painful. *Never again* to be here with us—never to sit with us at table, never to travel with us, never to laugh with us, never to cry with us, never to embrace us as he leaves for school, never to see his brothers and sisters marry. All the rest of our lives we must live without him.[1]

As a pastor for more than half a century, I can say from experience that one need not have reached the final third of life to feel the neverness of grief. Young, middle-aged, or elderly— all may be faced with the sense of overwhelming loss. But I can also confirm that virtually everyone in later life understands the fullness of neverness, has personally felt the emptiness and agonies of grief.

—Mary's Encounters with Grief and Joy—

In the Bible, one who had every right to have surprise-overload is Mary, the mother of Jesus. In Mary's lifetime, she moved from that which was expected to an intense turn into the unexpected.

Situations Never Expected

Luke's account of the birth of Jesus began with an angel coming to Mary. The angel announced that Mary would become the mother of the Messiah. In the words of the angel, "You have found favor with God" (Luke 1:30). Through only the touch of God's Holy Spirit, Mary would conceive. It sounds wonderful, and in truth, it was. We *still* are hushed by the miracle of it all.

But we usually overlook the practical ramifications of what this meant for Mary. She was suddenly an unwed mother. She nearly lost her fiancé, Joseph, who by law could have had her stoned. In Matthew's account of the birth of our Lord, Joseph is told what was going on. He was to take Mary as his wife, which would have been a very dangerous endeavor, but he did it.

What does Mary's story have to do with us? Like Mary, many of us will find ourselves in situations we could never have dreamed of or expected. It will take us a while to work through such unexpected joys and severe setbacks, but we need to remember that the Lord is with us every step of the way.

Matthew records how Herod, hearing a threat to his kingdom had been born (that threat being a baby boy named Jesus), set about seeking to find and destroy him. Joseph and Mary gathered their baby boy and fled to Egypt to escape Herod's desperate search, thrusting them into a strange land, far from home.

> *"The birth of Jesus took place like this. His mother, Mary, was engaged to be married to Joseph. Before they came to the marriage bed, Joseph discovered she was pregnant. (It was by the Holy Spirit, but he didn't know that.) Joseph, chagrined but noble, determined to take care of things quietly so Mary would not be disgraced. While he was trying to figure a way out, he had a dream. God's angel spoke in the dream: "Joseph, son of David, don't hesitate to get married. Mary's pregnancy is Spirit-conceived. God's Holy Spirit has made her pregnant."*
> —Matthew 1:18-20 MSG

Sometimes in life we find ourselves thrust into abrupt changes. Nothing seems comfortable or familiar. What's happening seems completely out of our control. Perhaps, as with Mary and Joseph, we are separated from family and friends at significant times in our lives.

> *"The Lord will guide you continually."*
> —Isaiah 58:11

During times like these, we can find support and strength in remembering that, wherever we are and whatever our circumstances, the Lord knows the way back home, just as he guided Mary and Joseph back home from Egypt.

Sorrow in Saying Good-bye

When Jesus was about thirty years old, the day came when he said good-bye to everything he knew as home. He left to be baptized by John and to begin his ministry. Mary knew it would never be the same again. There often can be grief in saying good-bye.

An Extended Family

As Jesus outgrew his Nazareth beginnings, a mother's worry may have grown steadily in Mary's heart. He was keeping an intense, exhausting schedule. She worried, as any mother would, for her son's well-being.

> *Like many people, Mary likely never had people in Nazareth or Jerusalem who understood what she was going through.*

One day, she sent her other children to bring Jesus home to rest for a while. When word reached him, Jesus's response was hard for a mother to take. He spread out his hands as if to include everyone and said, "*This* is my family."

Twenty centuries later, those of us who read those words feel included and even comforted. We feel as if we belong; our Lord Jesus Christ has claimed us as family. But imagine how Mary, *Jesus's mother*, must have felt. As far as we know, Jesus never went home to Nazareth again. For Mary the *neverness* of grief was very real and continued to grow.

> "*Then his mother and his brothers came; and standing outside, they sent to him and called him. A crowd was sitting around him; and they said to him, 'Your mother and your brothers and sisters are outside, asking for you.' And he replied, 'Who are my mother and my brothers?' And looking at those who sat around him, he said, 'Here are my mother and my brothers! Whoever does the will of God is my brother and sister and mother.'*"
>
> —Mark 3:31-35

When Death Comes

The day finally came when they arrested Jesus, tried him in the middle of the night, and Pilate relented to allow a crucifixion. That dreadful day we call Good Friday was not good for the disciples. For his mother Mary, it was devastating.

Where was she when he died? She and the other women were at the cross. The Scripture records that the disciples fled, but the women did not flee. The women, including Jesus's mother, stayed until the end (John 19:25).

Recent archeological discoveries give some correction to the traditional picture we have of Jesus on the cross. Their excavations have uncovered that the crosses were not nearly as tall as we picture them. Roman soldiers apparently made them only as tall as the condemned person. The person's feet would virtually be touching the ground. Mary would have been standing at eye level with Jesus, looking straight into the eyes of her son as he suffered and died.

> *"When Jesus saw his mother and the disciple whom he loved standing beside her, he said to his mother, 'Woman, here is your son.' Then he said to the disciple, 'Here is your mother.' And from that hour, the disciple took her into his own home."*
> —John 19:26-27

Of the twelve disciples, John did return to the crucifixion scene. Some of the last words Jesus spoke from the cross were to John and Mary: "Mary—this is your son; John—this is your mother." In other words, "Take care of each other." Soon thereafter, Jesus cried with a loud voice, "It is finished" (John 19:30). And Jesus died. As with all mothers who have lost sons, something within Mary also died.

In this heartbreaking story, the last nail is that Mary knew sorrow and grief as few can imagine. The Old Testament prophet wrote that the Messiah would be "a man of sorrows, and acquainted with grief" (Isaiah 53:3 ESV). He could have added, "so, too, will be his mother."

Women were there when Joseph of Arimathea and Nicodemus asked permission to take Christ's body down and bury him. Mary, along with the other women, watched it all and followed them to the grave. *Mary and the women were the first to arrive, the last to leave the cross, and the first to know where he was buried.*

Mary was there through all of the agony and suffering of the cross. Mary, the mother of Jesus, watched it all. Grief was a process she didn't avoid. Instead she journeyed through each painful stage alongside her son. If anyone had bereavement overload, it was Mary.

> As the prophets foretold, Jesus would be "a man of sorrows, and acquainted with grief" (Isaiah 53:3 ESV). They could have added, "so too will be his mother."

What about us? Grief is just as real for us. It can carve the word *sorrow* upon the soul. Consider Mary's pain watching her son die on a cross. Years before, she had heard the angel's promise that she would bear a son and He would save his people from their sins. But on that day of promise, little could she have known what a terrible, ugly, costly price her son Jesus would have to pay. Mary knew grief as few, if any, have known it since.

But Mary also came to experience that *grief never has the last word, unless we allow it.* Deep grief does not have an eraser. We never forget. But we do learn how to move beyond what has been to what can be.

—*Breakthrough*—

The Bible, as well as Mary, affirms that grief and loss do not have the last word. Resurrection and new life is possible even in the midst of the most painful grief. But how do we get there? *How do we move from a loss-oriented life back to our purpose-driven life?*

A distinguished grief-counseling scholar, J. William Worden, states that when we've suffered great loss, we tend to move back and forth between three circles: everyday life, loss-oriented life, and recovery. Sometimes we have control over which of these stages we're in. At other times, we don't. Grief can be overpowering at times.[2]

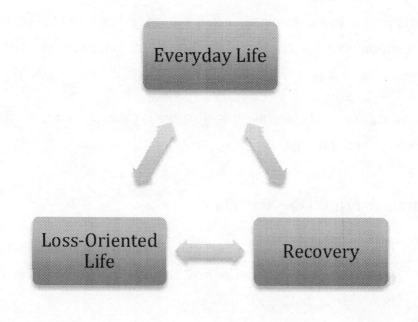

—*Living with Grief*—

After some unthinkable losses, we are immobilized—just like Mary. Something has died within us. As overwhelming grief begins, it's as if we don't care to live and are unable to face the day, much less the rest of our lives.

Part of the challenge is that our culture has little room for grief. In the past, a widow wore black for a year after the loss of a loved one. But today widows and widowers, like parents who have lost children, are expected to salute it all and in a few weeks walk on. And if, after a month or two, a person still grieves, the attitude is, *Get over it. Time to move on.* This is like a having a good friend fighting cancer and, after a single chemotherapy treatment, telling them, "Get over it. Move on."

There are many kinds of grief, but they have one thing in common: loss. Loss happens when we lose a job, when we retire, when we lose a spouse, and on and on. In life, grief happens.

During the early, frightening, disabling times of grief, many have found it helpful to live by three simple, practical rules:

Rule 1: Just Do the Next Thing

It sounds simple, but in traumatic loss, many people find it difficult to even get out of bed. Salute those who in heavy, heavy grief just *do the next thing.*

Why is doing the next thing so important? It employs the healing power of tasking. Each day take upon yourself a task or two that you don't feel like doing, don't want to do, but needs doing. Two good things happen. First, *things get done.* Second, *you give your emotions a rest* by *doing* something instead of *feeling* something. Tasking has healing power. Do the next thing.

Rule 2: Don't Expect Too Much of Yourself

Heavy grief takes a huge toll on one's physical and emotional strength. If you were physically disabled, you wouldn't expect yourself to function normally in just a few days. It might take weeks and months to heal the breaks, the wounds, and the disabilities. So with grief—it will take time. Don't expect too much of yourself.

Rule 3: Adopt an Attitude of Survival

This may sound strange in a world of high achievement. You may be a high achiever. But in heavy grief, remember you've been in an emotional train wreck, and it'll take a while for you to recover.

But sooner or later, you *will* begin to recover. You're like a wounded veteran back from war. You may never be as you once were. You may walk with a limp from now on. But you will begin to deal with it and get on with your life.

That's the way it is with heavy grief. You may walk with an emotional limp the rest of your life. But the time will come, perhaps not as soon as you would like, when you want to get on with your life. In some small way, you will want to move from surviving to thriving.[3]

—The Spiritual Medicines of Recovery—

So you've taken the first step. You've begun to understand the healing power of tasking. You've learned how to survive, and now you're ready to sustain the gains you've made. The question is, of course, how do you keep moving forward instead of sliding back into depressive patterns? Establishing rituals and symbols, transforming your loss into a tribute, and using and accessing your faith will allow you to move forward.

Using and Accessing Your Faith

In the early days of loss, most of us are numb. We may seek comfort in our Bibles or in the kind words of friends, but we are usually too overwhelmed by loss to find the healing that we need. But make no mistake: faith is in action. There is a ministry of presence—those who are there for us, propping us up, carrying us through, bringing a meal, helping us navigate things that have to be done. It may be as simple as one who persistently but patiently encourages us to get out of bed, to get out of the house, to steadily get through our grief. Hopefully as time passes we can access our faith in our daily walk, beyond tearful prayers of grief.

Find some Scriptures that comfort your heart and quote them again and again. Many people have come to treasure Deuteronomy 31:8: "It is the Lord who goes before you. He will be with you; he will not fail you or forsake you. Do not fear or be dismayed."

This is what happened to Mary and the disciples. The hurt and terror of the cross was replaced by the resurrection. They realized that what was happening on that cross was crucial for the healing of all of us, but they also grasped the eternal truth that life transcends death.

Eventually loss and grief lose their power to rule our actions and emotions, but it can take a long time. Mary journeyed from grief at the foot of the cross—trusting, transforming it to a symbol of hope and faith.

Rituals and Symbols

To honor and pay tribute to the person you've lost, you may find it helpful to come up with rituals that remember the person with hope and promise. Invent some rituals that embrace what was, but look forward to what can be.

A woman who lost her husband came up with a set of activities that are a tribute to what they did together. These rituals have their roots in the times they gardened together. When the flowers bloom, when the vegetables come through the surface of the garden, it is not only a tribute to what they used to do together, but also a symbol of hope for new life in spite of such painful loss.

"In our house, Shirley lights a candle every Sunday for our son Dave. When we light the candle, it is a tribute and a remembrance of Dave and what he means to us, a symbol of hope, promise, and light."

—Peter James Flamming

Transform Your Loss into a Tribute

Grief involves some changes in the way we look at things. One important change is the process of transforming grief feelings into a tribute.

> *Grief can become like an inner physician.*

Begin to see grief as a healer, even a friend. Like a physician, as grief heals it will begin to ask some important *healing questions:*

- **Would you really like to walk on as if nothing has happened?**
- **Would you really like to be able to forget the person for whom you grieve and erase him or her from your memory?**
- **Would you really like to live as if that person's place in your life didn't matter?**
- **Would you really like to move through anniversaries and holidays as if that person never existed?**

The answer to each one of these questions would probably, and almost certainly, be … *no.*

You may find that the soft wisdom of grief whispers, "Don't you see that *part of the intense pain of your grief is your tribute to the one you have loved and lost?* It's your salute to a life well lived, a commendation and blessing for the one you remember with such devotion."

When you find yourself immobilized or overcome by grief, stop for a while. In your mind, realize that the deep feelings of loss wouldn't be there if that person didn't mean so much to you. Grief can often become the first step toward a deep heart-felt tribute. You wouldn't feel so deeply if you did not honor him or her so much.

CHAPTER 9

The John Discovery:
Crescendo to Life's Last Note

Then they said to him, 'What must we do to perform the work of God?' Jesus answered them, 'This is the work of God, that you believe in him whom he has sent.'
—John 6:28–29

The John Discovery

Crescendo to Life's Last Note

—Transforming Aloneness—

Musical composer Franz Liszt's saw the natural fulfillment of his lifelong spiritual commitment when he lived for several years in a simple monastic cell in Rome in his later years. Here in 1865, his prolific choral output reached its peak and continues to be explored today.

To quote Liszt's biographer, Alan Walker, "Nothing is more remarkable in all Liszt's creative output than the pieces he composed in the last decade of his life. If he had written nothing else, he would still be an extraordinary composer."[1]

Like Liszt the composer, John the disciple of Jesus lived to be an older man, the last man standing among the twelve. He found extraordinary power contained in his later years. He may be the ultimate centenarian, vibrantly living to over one hundred years old. John wasn't sitting on a front porch in a rocking chair withering away. Instead we see an older, wiser John, whose hope burned brightly right up until the last. His Gospel was probably written in his later years.

Of the four Gospels, John's is unique. Matthew, Mark, and Luke recorded what have become known as the Synoptic Gospels because they can be compared side-

> *John could have focused on drowning in loneliness, but instead he chooses an entirely different perspective.*

by-side. John presents miracles Jesus performed that don't appear in the other Gospels. And his focus is less on the narrative story and the teachings we need to follow than it is on who Jesus was. Perhaps because John knew what the earlier Gospels revealed, he decided to give us a different story—a very intimate look at the last days in the life of Christ, especially the last twenty–four hours, including the resurrection (John 13–21).

Why is this important to us? John's Gospel focuses on how we can grow spiritually in Christ, no matter what age we are. John helps us understand how Christ can assist us during difficult times and reminds us that He will *never leave us nor forsake us.* This is especially true in our last days, months, and years.

John records seven "I am" statements of Jesus. These statements identify two crucial spiritual realities. First, the statements clarify what Jesus is about. He is like a mirror to show what God is like. The second is to describe His purpose on earth on our behalf. He uses simple but crucial images, most of them familiar in our daily lives. This allows us to readily connect with what Jesus is talking about, even after two thousand years.

I am the Bread of Life (John 6:35, 41, 48, 51)
I am the Light of the world (John 8:12)
I am the Gate [or the Door] (John 10:7, 9)
I am the Good Shepherd (John 10:11, 14)
I am the Resurrection and the Life (John 11:25)
I am the Way, the Truth, and the Life (John 14:6)
I am the Vine, you are the branches (John 15:5)

The "I am" statements are *not a list of dos and don'ts.* The spiritual life isn't about keeping a set of religious rules but is an *invitation to a spiritual experience.* The spiritual reality comes through a personal relationship, a vital and eternal relationship with God as we know and understand Him through Jesus Christ.

To say it another way, the "I am" declarations of our Lord are relational and spiritual statements, not regulating statements. Jesus gives us ways in which He wants to connect with us relationally and spiritually. What John helps us see through these images is who Jesus is and what He is about. The images remain relevant for every age and culture.

Most important, John helps us understand the vital relationship between Jesus Christ, the Messiah, and God's Holy Spirit, that mysterious inner voice that speaks to our hearts and guides us on our spiritual journey. John's gospel makes it clear that Jesus and the Holy Spirit work together in concert. They are separate but overlapping influences in our lives.

Think of this relationship in terms of modern musical notation. In piano and organ music, for example, there are two parts: the treble and base clefts. On each musical line, these two are usually joined together even though they don't play the same notes. In many ways, the two clefts are similar. They are in the same musical key, using the same musical notes although in different combinations. They often use portions of the same chords yet both clefts are different. In playing the piano, what the right hand does isn't the same as the left hand, yet they come together to make the same music. Without both of them, the music isn't the same. This explains the two-fold emphasis John has on Jesus Christ, on the one hand, and the Holy Spirit on the other.

Jesus' timeless redemptive work in the world is the same spiritual music that the Holy Spirit brings to our lives. The two are different, but they make the same music. When they are in concert working together, redemptive miracles happen. To help us understand how Jesus enters our lives through the Holy

Spirit, John gives us some common, everyday words—words that take on deeply spiritual meanings.

—*The Gatekeeper*—

Twice in the tenth chapter of John's Gospel, Jesus calls himself "the gate," a phrase often translated as "the door." John beautifully articulates that God is right where we are. God is not so busy running the universe that individual persons are overlooked. Jesus said, "I stand at the door and knock" (Revelation 3:20). Jesus is trying to get our attention.

A famous painting of this beautiful image by artist Warner Sallman depicts Jesus outside a rather heavy-looking door. Jesus is knocking. The painting shows He's present, but He is not entering until He is invited to do so. The door must be opened from the inside.

John opened himself up to be useful when it seemed that his days had passed. Like John, we face this decision in our later life. Will we make ourselves available and open to the risen Lord? He desires to fill us with His spirit and use us for His purposes and for our fulfillment. But we have to say yes to God.

John must have also wrestled with being alone and lonely. In countless retirement communities and nursing homes, I have met people who feel the dull, endless ache of loneliness, of feeling old and ignored. John himself surely felt this way as he approached the 100-year mark. He could have simply accepted it as inevitable—and fallen into self-pity. In a real sense, he was alone. His brother, the disciple James, had been a martyr for Jesus fifty years before John wrote his Gospel. The other disciples had all died, as had virtually all of John's friends.

But John refused to accept his final years as useless. Instead, he took full advantage of his free time and put together the Gospel we enjoy today. He transformed his "alone-ness" into purposeful living. That transformation is "The John Discovery"—the lesson that tells us we are never too old to be useful to God and to those around us.

The choice is ours. Will we open ourselves to the possibility of establishing a spiritual relationship with God, through Jesus Christ the living Lord and the work of the Holy Spirit? Will we find His purpose for our later lives? The important picture we need to etch permanently on our memory is of the Lord knocking at the door. He will enter only when *we choose* to let Him in. This is a choice we will need to make not only at the beginning of our spiritual journey, but often.

Haven't you heard someone say, "I came to a desperate place and suddenly realized I hadn't shared any of this with the Lord. I needed to bring Him into it." In a spiritual sense, our Lord never leaves once we invite His spirit into our lives. But in an intellectual and rational sense, we often seal him out. We become preoccupied with our problems. Then we remember Jesus. We discover once again that we don't work our way to

Him. He has already worked His way to us. He is the door, but we have to open it.

—*The Good Shepherd*—

Jesus tells us, *"I am the good shepherd. The Good Shepherd lays down his life for the sheep"* (John 10:11). Jesus contrasts Himself with a hired hand who, at the first sight of danger, runs away and vanishes. Not so the Good Shepherd. He will be there for us, even to the point of laying down His life for us—just as He did on the cross.

It is no coincidence that John, a man seemingly alone in the world, would be the one to tell of the Good Shepherd. John had experienced the presence of Jesus coming to him as a Spiritual Shepherd. In the spiritual journey, there are times of great joy, confidence, and a great sense of overcoming. There are other times when we struggle. Jesus says, "Like a shepherd, I will be there for you. Regardless of the difficulties you are going through, I will be there with you and for you. Like a good shepherd is there for his sheep, I will be there for you."

Now that you have the freedom to choose how to spend your time, spend some time with the Good Shepherd. Weigh the

> *Christ has promised to be there with us, as a shepherd is for his sheep.*

possibilities, the pluses and the minuses of every decision, through prayer. Then wait. Give it time. Sometimes the answer doesn't come at once, which probably means this isn't a "good versus bad" decision, and you need time to work through it. If you give it time, the answer will come. *The important thing is to share these decision times with the Lord.*

In our later years, we especially need a Good Shepherd. In these times we are often forced to deal with illness and even critical surgeries. Jesus will walk with us all of the way. He is the Good Shepherd who suffered on the cross. He knows what it is to suffer and to face difficult choices.

—*Characteristics of Jesus as Our Shepherd*—

Jesus, as the Good Shepherd, showed characteristics of mercy, cross-bearing, and peace. These three dimensions of His love carry us into a deeper and more meaningful relationship with Him.

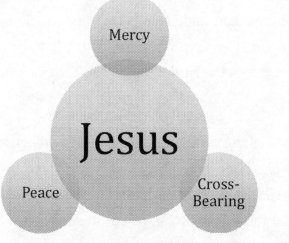

Mercy

In his later years, John was able to give special attention to how the risen Christ comes to us, often in the tugs and pulls of life. For instance, in John's Gospel (chapter 4), Jesus is on His way back to Galilee. On the way, He had to journey through Samaria. He stopped near Jacob's well to get a drink of water. A Samaritan woman was drawing water. He asked if she would give Him some water. She was shocked. "You are a Jew, and I am a Samaritan woman. How can you ask me for a drink?" Jesus, using water as a metaphor to bridge the spiritual gap between them, speaks to her about *living water*, which brings eternal life. She says she wants that living water but has no idea what He is talking about.

Jesus asks her to bring her husband, to which she replies she has no husband. Jesus says, "You are right when you say you have no husband. The fact is, that you have had five husbands, and the man you now have is not your husband" (John 4:17–18 NIV). The woman understands that Jesus is no ordinary man but a prophet. She then responds with what she knows about the difference between the Samaritan religion and the Jewish religion.

Jesus erases these differences completely with these remarkable words: "The hour is coming, and is now here, when the true worshipers will worship the Father in spirit and truth … God is spirit, and those who worship him must worship in spirit and truth." The woman, wise beyond her experiences in life, speaks of a Messiah who will come and explain everything. Jesus responds by saying, "I who speak to you am he" (John 4:23– 24, 26).

In its setting, this is truly a remarkable conversation! Why? Not only because it is a conversation between a Samaritan and a Jew (forbidden), and a man and

> *Jesus not only lets the woman know who He is, but He blends in His work with the Spirit's work.*

a woman (forbidden), but also because Jesus chooses to reveal who He is and what His life is about to a woman whose life has been a disaster. This is mercy in real life.

Peace

Peace is a word used in many ways and to describe many events. But John portrays a different kind of peace: an inner peace. That kind of peace was significant to John, because his outward appearance—often described as loving and tranquil—masked an inner turmoil and temper that, when he was pushed to the limit, could burst forth with startling force. Indeed, in his early years, John and his brother (and fellow disciple) James were nicknamed the "sons of thunder."

But in his later days, John received the gift of the Holy Spirit, and that gift gave him

> *The Apostle John found inner peace in his later life.*

inner peace. John records that, after the resurrection, Jesus's first words to his disciples were, "Peace be with you." His second words were, "Peace be with you." A week later, when doubting Thomas finally beheld the risen Lord, Jesus's first words to Thomas were, "Peace be with you." Safe to say that inner peace was important to Jesus! John also writes that Jesus breathed on his disciples and, in doing so, breathed the gift of the Holy Spirit into their hearts and souls. The Spirit gave John the peace that Jesus was hoping he would find (John 20:19, 21, 22, 26).

The word *peace* and the Holy Spirit go together. John, one of the sons of thunder, had found peace within himself through the Holy Spirit, and he sought to give the gift of inner peace to others.

Cross-Bearing

Unlike the other three gospels, John's Gospel fastens its primary attention on the last days and hours of our Lord. Part of John's account relates the time Jesus spent teaching His disciples. It's as if the Lord

> When our Lord asks us to bear our crosses, He does not ask us to do what He didn't do. His cross- bearing dwarfs ours. Whatever we go through, it shrinks when we compare it to what our Lord went through.

knew His time was short, and He was trying to teach his disciples everything possible.

A major portion of Jesus's final teaching deals with the cross, the one He will carry and die upon, and those we will be asked to carry. When the time came for Jesus to bear His cross, John recorded what happened: "So the soldiers took charge of Jesus. Carrying his own cross, he went out to the place of the Skull (which in Aramaic is Golgotha). There they crucified him, and with him two others—one on each side and Jesus in the middle" (John 19:16–18 NIV).

We have, as Christians, made the cross the prime symbol of our faith. The cross is found in virtually every church and is often the centerpiece of our worship. Jesus on the cross adorns our stained-glass windows. For Jesus, it was a real cross. The crown they placed on His head was not a crown made for a king, but a crown of thorns, a cruel sign of disgrace.

John records that Pilate had a notice prepared and fastened to the cross. It read: *Jesus of Nazareth, The King of the Jews*, written in Aramaic (the language of the people of Israel), Latin, and Greek.

(Aramaic) يسوع الناصري ملك اليهود
Iesus Nazarenus Rex Iudaeorum (Latin)
Ἰησοῦς ὁ Ναζωραῖος ὁ βασιλεὺς τῶν Ἰουδαίων (Greek)

These three languages have two significant symbolic meanings. The *first* is that the cross of Christ is for everyone, everywhere. It's for royalty as well as for regular workers, the sophisticated set and the common people. The second is that the cross is meant for the whole world, not just for one nationality or one religious segment, for it was written in the three most widely used languages of that day. His cross is for the whole world.

Should you be reading these words during a period of great suffering, sense the presence of the suffering Savior right along with you. Feel the companionship of the One who has been there. Jesus taught that we would be called upon to bear our own crosses. "If any want to become my followers, let them deny themselves and take up their cross, and follow me" (Mark 8:34). Our Lord speaks very clearly about us bearing our own crosses and following him. What does it meant to bear your own cross?

More than two hundred years ago, the French Archbishop Francois Fenelon taught about the spiritual impact of cross bearing. In a letter he wrote:

Dear friend,

You're going to have some crosses to carry in your life. And you better get ready for it. These are your options. You can complain about it. You can wish it wasn't there. You can pretend it's not there. You can run away from it. Or you can pick it up and you can carry it like Jesus carried his cross. And when you do you're going to look over to the side and there's Jesus carrying his cross right alongside of you. And if you stumble remember he stumbled also on the way to Golgotha.

Then, something's going to happen to you. When you're willing to carry your cross as your own and in partnership with Jesus to say, 'I'm part of his team and I'm joining him,' it changes you. Something happens inside. You get strength beyond yourself to carry it.[2]

The change of heart when you bear your own cross takes you to a new spiritual level. When you bear your own suffering, your own cross, for Jesus's sake, often a peace that surpasses understanding comes from above and settles in the soul. It is a transformation within both your mind and your heart. If you try to understand bearing your own cross as an intellectual doctrine, you may miss it completely. If you let it pierce your inner soul at a deep level, you may not be able to put it into words, but you'll experience a oneness with Christ you may never have had before. *Picture Him bearing His cross, and then invite Him to help you carry yours.*

CHAPTER 10

The Naomi & Ruth Discovery:
Courage to Take the Next Step

Where you die I will die, and there will I be buried. May the Lord do so to me and more also if anything but death parts me from you.

—Ruth 1:17 ESV

The Naomi & Ruth Discovery

Courage to Take the Next Step

Naomi rose early one morning to watch the sunrise. She was remembering the days when her life had been more in rhythm with the meaning of her name: "pleasant, delight and loveliness."[1]

Before the famine came with such intensity, life had seemed so full of joy and promise. She had married the love of her life, Elimelech. They had been blessed with two wonderful sons, Mahlon and Chilion. She remembered the wonderful days when they were younger and she would carry them around in her arms.

The famine changed everything, making everyone a refugee from happiness. Usually dry spells ended with the rains bathing the thirsty land. Everyone had believed that the rains would come. They had been through dry spells before. The feeling was, "It will rain, you will see. We must be ready to work hard when the storms come."

But the rainy season quickly came *and* just as quickly went. Famine became the dreaded reality. No crops to harvest meant no food to eat. Gardens that once filled the tables with more than enough food for the family now lay barren.

Elimelech tossed and turned at night, trying to work things out in his mind as he wrestled with what was best for his family. Since family was the most important thing in his life, he couldn't risk staying in Bethlehem if it meant starvation for his wife and sons. He had to move where it rained and his family would have food to eat.

He decided to move to Moab. Why Moab? Jews hated the Moabites. But desperate situations lead to unusual solutions. Moab, because of its location and elevation, *always* had rain and *always* had food.

After a wretched night's sleep, Elimelech sat down with his wife, Naomi, to share his heart and his decision. His prejudice against Moabites was real and intense, but the resolve to save his family was even greater. Imagine him talking it over with Naomi, saying, perhaps with a quivering voice, "I think we must move to Moab. I hate it. If there were any other option, I would take it. But if we stay, we will starve to death. I love you and the boys more than anything on the face of the earth. That the three of you survive is more important than my feelings about the Moabites. We cannot stay where we are." So Elimelech and Naomi *took the next step*—they moved to Moab.

For Elimelech's family, this would be just the beginning of many such canyons that would require them to realize they couldn't do the perfect thing; they could only do the next thing.

> *The canyons of uncertainty in life can't be crossed by figuring everything out but only by taking the next step.*

—The Family in Moab—

In Moab, Elimelech and his family found a place to live and began to settle in. In truth, it all went better than they had expected. Her sons, Mahlon and Chilion, made friends easily. Elimelech found work and fit in reluctantly but well. Most important, they had food to eat.

Naomi must have lived with mixed emotions. On the one hand, Moab was beginning to feel like home. She was pleased that Mahlon and Chilion were fitting in. As they grew older she really struggled as they began to date Moabite girls. What if they fell in love and married one of these girls?

She would soon find her intuition was right on target. Mahlon fell in love with a Moabite girl named Ruth. Before she could even begin to get comfortable with the Moabite culture, Naomi had to plan and celebrate a wedding.

Perhaps Naomi and Elimelech hoped that before Chilion fell in love and married, the famine in Bethleham would break, the rains would return, and they could return home. But it was not to be. After Mahlon married Ruth, Chilion fell in love with Orpah, a Moabite, and also married. So instead of moving back to their homeland, their sons were rooted even more deeply in the city of Moab.

Not long after their sons' nuptials, another tragedy came in the form of a dreadful disease of epidemic proportions. As it swept

> *The unthinkable happened. Ruth, Naomi and Orpah all became widows.*

across Moab, it seemed to immediately strike the men. The first to get sick was Elimelech. Then Mahlon and Chilion. The disease took its toll; all three died as the epidemic took the lives of countless men in Moab. This brought the unthinkable: Ruth, Naomi and Orpah all became widows. Grief knew no boundaries, and all three women experienced deep sorrow.

Of course, grief was no stranger to Naomi. She had felt its first deep sting when they left Bethlehem and moved to Moab. She had lost her family, her friends, and her home. And surely she experienced her own private agony when her sons married Moabite women. But even that was nothing like what she was facing now. Her husband was gone. Both of her sons were gone. She was left alone with only the Moabite wives of her sons. Widows survived in those days by depending upon family. Ruth and Orpah had families in Moab. Naomi had no one.

—*The Rains Return*—

Years later, Naomi received word the rains had returned in Bethlehem. There would be a harvest season there. She could return to family and friends. But she was no longer young, and the journey would be difficult. Could she find the energy to make the long walk from Moab to Bethlehem on her own? She decided to try.

Saying good-bye to her daughters-in-law, Ruth and Orpah, was more difficult than she had imagined. They wanted to go with her, a strong testament to

> *Perhaps in the secret place of her own heart, Naomi felt God leading her to return to Bethlehem.*

Naomi's influence on these young women. They had watched her, learned from her, loved her, and now they wanted to follow her, even if it meant leaving the only place they had called home. And in the end, they decided to go with her. The three started out together, but Naomi realized that Ruth and Orpah, these Moabite women, would be submitting themselves to hatred and distain in Bethlehem. She felt she must go alone; she insisted they return.

She reasoned with them. Her best days were gone, but they still had productive lives to lead. "My daughters, it has been far more bitter for me than for you, because the hand of the Lord has turned against me" (Ruth 1:13).

Naomi had been "seasoned by tragedy and enlivened by her own stubborn faith," Marjory Bankson writes in *Seasons of Friendship*. Most of us wouldn't be able to bear removing what we felt was our last shoulder to cry on and people to journey alongside. But Naomi's strong courage came to the fore. As much as she needed their presence, she was willing to release it.[2]

Then came the surprise. Again, Ruth and Orpah insisted on traveling with Naomi—they felt they must stay together. But once again, Naomi insisted Ruth and Orpah must stay in Moab. Their roots were there, their family. More important, they were Gentiles and wouldn't be accepted in Bethlehem.

But Ruth knew Naomi needed her and that in some way, being there for her would make the difference. *She stepped out in love.* So in spite of Naomi's effort to persuade her to stay with her own people and in her own land, Ruth refused to leave Naomi's side. In the words of the Scripture, "Ruth clung to her" (Ruth 1:14).

> *What is Love?*
> *"It is not an affectionate feeling, but a steady wish for the loved person's ultimate good as far as it can be obtained."*
> —C. S. Lewis

Again and again Naomi pleaded with her to stay with her people. But Ruth replied with these unforgettable words: "Do not press me to leave you or to turn back from following you! Where you go, I will go; where you lodge, I will lodge; your people shall be my people, and your God my God" (Ruth 1:16).

Ruth became a lovely friend to Naomi at a critical time in her life. Along with Naomi, Ruth would set her face toward Judah. In Bethlehem they would have to encourage each other in the challenging days ahead.

—*Winter Season*—

Even though some time had passed since the deaths of Naomi's husband and sons, she and Ruth were still in a winter season emotionally. Most of us have, or will likely, experience a loss we simply cannot handle. The skill, determination, knowledge, and willpower that has worked in the past will be rendered ineffective. In effect, we will be led to the edge of our resources. Some call this period in our lives *winter*. It's a time when we feel the cold icy reality that life seems to have turned against us.

In *Seasons of Friendship,* Marjory Bankson writes about the season of winter in her poem, "Circle of Seasons":

**winter
season of me
of solitude and silence
drawing on reserves
dimly seen**[3]

The picture of two widows, Naomi and Ruth, walking along the shoreline of the Dead Sea toward Judah, epitomized winter.

Even though a traveling pair, the two very much had individual journeys and struggles to work though.

During these difficult times, we may need a friend, a winter friend. A winter friend may be an old friend who's undergoing a major change in his or her life. Or it may be someone entirely new, someone often older, who's been there and knows how to be there when others are in need.

> *A winter season of our lives may happen simply because we're spiritual creatures and our souls need time to rest and renew from the inside out.*

We may have experienced a wintery season early in life, but in our later years, the number of losses—both relational and personal—calls for extraordinary inner resources. Richard Rohr, author of *Falling Upward*, puts it this way: "Our mature years are defined by a kind of bright sadness and a sober happiness … there is still darkness in the second half of life, in fact maybe even more. But now there is a changed capacity to hold it creatively and with less anxiety."[4]

—*Journeying Beyond Herself*—

Why did Ruth make the decision to continue with Naomi in spite of the difficulties she would face when she arrived in a Jewish land? Perhaps Ruth, in wisdom and even revelation beyond herself, realized she was not the only one who mattered. Even though she was seared by loss and disappointment, *Ruth made a pledge to Naomi* in a way that marked the beginning of a lifelong friendship.

Jane Brody of New York had been married forty-four years when her husband died. Confronting a steep learning curve about finances and other tasks her husband had taken care of, and surrounded by family and friends who made sure she stayed busy, the first year of widowhood passed in a kind of numb blur. Then came year number two, and things got worse. The family moved on and assumed she had too. Deep sadness and loneliness set in. Therapy helped, but it did not fill the void. As she put it, "There was an emptiness that may be hard to understand unless you've also been through it."

Then Brody stumbled upon John Robbins' best-selling book, *Healthy at 100*, and things improved. She took special interest in Robbins' section on relationships. Robbins struck a chord with Jane Brody when, as she explained, he writes about "the importance of others in our lives and takes issue with self-absorption, with the 'me' generation that focuses on itself to the neglect of others." She continued:

Robbins cites an illustrative study published in 1983 by Larry Scherwitz, then a psychologist at Baylor University, who taped the conversations of nearly 600 men, a third of them with heart disease. Dr. Scherwitz counted how often the men used first-person pronouns—I, me, mine—and found *that those who used them most often were most likely to have heart disease and, when followed for several years, most likely to suffer heart attacks.* The psychologist advised: "Listen with regard when others talk. Give your time and energy to others; let others have their way; do things for reasons other than furthering your own needs."

Brody did listen, and she determined that she needed "something that connects me more directly to people I care about."[5]

Focusing on the needs of others! That is key. As Brody wrote, "Time for me to get out of myself." How? Build a new social network. Hold on to an established friendship.

> *"Faith is taking the next step when you can't see the whole staircase."*
> —Martin Luther King, Jr.

Join a cause one believes in. The result? Less sadness and better health. Robbins and Brody could have been writing about the needs of Ruth or Naomi. The research of Dr. Scherwitz should bring a useful and essential pause in the decisions about our lives. *If we make our decisions only with ourselves in mind, we might want to take a look at our crucial relationships. We may need to establish or reestablish connections that will make all the difference in the days ahead.* It made all of the difference for Ruth to think beyond herself to the welfare of Naomi. It turned out not only to be the best for Naomi but also for Ruth.

—*The Next Step*—

Neither Ruth nor Naomi knew what the first step would be when they arrived in Bethlehem. Both stepped out in faith and courage. Diane Barth, author of *Daydreaming: Unlock the Creative Power of Your Mind*, states in the July 2011 issue of *Psychology Today*, "The faith you need is the belief that if you take the first step, the second one will become accessible. With each one, subsequent steps become a bit more manageable. The steps may not always seem to go in a straight line, or even to take you forward."[6]

Naomi and Ruth arrive in Judah, but Ruth is a Moabite in a country that hates Moabites. Although Naomi stands by her, Ruth has no money, no food, and no way to earn a living. *What does one do when everything that was planned for and depended upon is suddenly gone?*

Ruth takes the only available path—gleaning. Gleaning was the only means of survival for the poorest of the poor. It required laboring behind the harvesters and servants to gather the remaining stalks of grain after the harvest.

At midday, Boaz, the landowner, looked across the field and his gaze stopped on Ruth. He asked, "Who is this young woman? Where did she come from?"

> *"As the God of Israel has gathered you under his wings, you have there found refuge."*
>
> —Ruth 2:12

His foreman answered, "Why, that's the Moabite girl, the one who came with Naomi from the country of Moab."

Boaz later approached Ruth and said, "I've given orders to my servants not to harass you. When you get thirsty, feel free to go and drink from the water buckets that the servants have filled." Being treated as a servant was a real bonus for Ruth. As a servant she got water and lunch. Knowing the customs of the day, Ruth bowed down before him and said, "How does this happen that you should pick me out and treat me so kindly—me, a foreigner?"

Boaz answered her, "I've heard all about you—heard about the way you treated your mother-in-law after the death of her husband, and how you left your father and mother and the land of your birth and have come to live among total strangers. God will reward you well for what you've done" (Ruth 2:5–6, 9–12).

Ruth was willing to glean, taking the next step that came with a myriad of vulnerabilities. Despite that, in the process Boaz saw something more in Ruth. The seeds of a future love relationship were planted.

After talking things over, Naomi convinced Ruth to take the next step. When the night came, Ruth was to go and sleep at the feet of Boaz and when he awoke he would find her there. By this action, Boaz would know that, even though she was a foreigner, she hadn't gone after any of the young men, whether rich or poor. When she said, "Spread your cloak over your maidservant," she made it clear that she had chosen him.

Boaz sensed her insecurity and apprehension, but he reassured Ruth that she was *not* about to lose her honor, nor her future.

Often overlooked in this sensitive love story is the behind-the-scenes work of Naomi on behalf of both Ruth and Boaz. Both proved responsive to the

> *Both Naomi and Ruth are able to use their unique situations in life on behalf of the other.*

instructions that Naomi had given to them. Ruth is rightly given the credit for being a key person in the lineage of David and of Christ. But none of this would have happened had Naomi not been the arranger, almost a coach if you will. She provided the needed council and guidance for Ruth in this crucial time in her life.

Two generations meet in this story. Redemption happens for both Ruth and Naomi. Why? Because the two are able to use their unique situations in life on behalf of the other. Their intergenerational features can serve as a model for us. Often the older generation gravitates to those of their age group, and they should. But sensitivity to the Ruths of the younger generation can be like discovering new family. Blessings are realized by both generations.

Naomi is for Ruth what Ruth cannot be for herself. And eventually Ruth is for Naomi what Naomi cannot be for herself. Seared by their mutual losses and disappointments, Ruth made a pledge to Naomi in a way that marked the beginning of a lifetime friendship.

Whether men or women, we're *all* like Naomi and Ruth. We need someone who's like family to us when our original family can no longer be there.

On that significant night when Ruth and Boaz were brought together by the instruction and planning of Naomi, scandal was a real possibility. But Ruth knew, just as Naomi knew, that

> *There are times when we need someone who is willing to lift us up when we need it or let us lift them up when they need it.*

what she most needed was a kinsman redeemer.

—The Kinsman Redeemer—

Ruth needed what was considered in her time as a "kinsman redeemer," a person who would claim the destitute and abandoned and make them part of the family.

The "redeemer" ideal denoted that although the person was not a blood relative, they were claimed as family. They now belonged. Christians believe that this is a beautiful picture of what Christ does for us.

Boaz became Ruth's kinsman redeemer. He became her kinsman because he married her. He became her redeemer because she had no family and he made her family.

What Boaz did in a local sense, Jesus Christ did in an eternal sense. Coming as the Son of God, He made us *kin* in the family of God. As God, He becomes our redeemer. As man, He lifts us up and makes us part of God's family.

The lives of both Naomi and Ruth have a recurring theme of darkness. Heartbreak upon heartbreak happens in such a way that no one really recovers from one before they must face another. Darkness is real. Sorrow and uncertainty are real. But darkness never completely snuffs out the light.

> *The incredible life and destiny of Ruth is light in the midst of darkness.*

In Naomi's most desperate hour, Ruth will not leave her. In Ruth's most desperate hour, Naomi returns the favor. Naomi uses her wisdom, born of life's hard knocks, to boost Ruth's prospects. *Taking the next step, doing the next thing, does not mean the end of the story. It may just be the beginning of a new story.* That's what it came to mean for Ruth.

Boaz steps in and claims Ruth; he loves her and marries her. Through the actions of Naomi, Boaz helps Ruth take the next step. She not only becomes part of his family, but also becomes the mother of Obed, who becomes the father of Jesse, who becomes the father of David—who becomes King of Israel. When the Moabite Ruth became the bride of Boaz, it caused quite a stir in Judah! But God was at work in Boaz's unusual, if not scandalous, choice. Out of the darkness of Naomi's and Ruth's lives came the light of the world.

Kindness is that incredible bridge that allows Naomi and Ruth to turn from the hardships of what had been to the possibilities that could be. *Kindness was the bridge from hurt to healing.* Kindness is that gift that one friend gives to another friend that allows them to turn their gaze from the past to a hopeful glimpse of the future.

In a recent commencement address at Syracuse University, George Saunders, a middle-aged writer and professor who is wise beyond his years, listed a number of things that most older people might regret as they look backward. He views them as part of his regret memory. What he regretted most, curiously enough, was his lack of kindness (not even outright meanness) toward a shy new kid in school. She wore "blue cat's eye glasses that, at that time, only old ladies wore." The kids made fun of her, which made her visibly sad. Soon she moved away. This mild incident of incivility still bothers Saunders, because in it he recognized a larger human tendency to forget the importance of kindness in making anyone's life worthwhile and the world a better place. As he said to the graduates, *"What I regret most in my life are failures of human kindness."* But all was not lost, he added. "One thing in our favor: some of this 'becoming kinder' happens naturally, with age. It might be a simple matter of attrition: as we get older, we come to see how useless it is to be selfish—how illogical, really."[7]

What can help us be kinder? Among Saunders' answers: education, art, prayer, meditation, and friendship. But he concluded the list with the suggestion of "establishing ourselves in some kind of spiritual tradition—recognizing that there have been countless really smart people before us who have asked these same questions and left behind answers for us." Recognize the trailblazers. Take note of people whose lives have shown a deep spirituality and an unusual willingness to push forward the boundaries of kindness.

Naomi and Ruth both left those kinds of trails for us to follow. We see their unwavering commitment to a friendship that, in itself, would benefit neither woman. Both had discovered the necessity of taking the next step, and, despite all the tragedies and difficulties that befell them, they became kinder, not meaner. We too must learn to take the next step. May we understand the importance of kindness as we move ahead.

In your life, you may be at the doorstep where a courage beyond yourself will be required. Consider the connections between Naomi and Ruth and yourself, between the everyday challenges they confronted and the everyday challenges you are confronting now. Do you hear the echoes of their lives in the challenges you are facing? As you think on these things, ask yourself these questions:

1. Will you take the next steps despite a great loss?
2. Will you embark on the journey despite so many unknowns?
3. Will you think beyond how you expect things will turn out?
4. Will you see the opportunity to provide wise counsel?
5. Will you seek the opportunity to seek wise counsel?
6. What situation in your life needs redemption?

CHAPTER 11

The David Discovery:

Five Smooth Stones for Facing Challenge

*Count it all joy, my brothers, when you meet
trials of various kinds, for you know that the
testing of your faith produces steadfastness.
And let steadfastness have its full
effect, that you may be perfect and
complete, lacking in nothing.*
—James 1:2–4 ESV

The David Discovery

Five Smooth Stones for Facing Challenge

David is one of the central personalities in the Bible. His life story is told in the Old Testament: First and Second Samuel. Although Samuel has a key part in these two books, they are really David's books, and they might just as well be called First David and Second David. The fact of the matter is there is more about David and his life in the Bible than any other character. However, the influence of his life reaches far beyond the Old Testament narrative. His tenure as king established Jerusalem as the capital city of the Jewish nation, bringing a divided nation together.

Bethlehem, the city of David, was the place Jesus was born. Over seventy of the one hundred and fifty Psalms are attributed to David and reflect both the poet and the musician that resided in his mind and soul.

David's life and psalms serve as a primer on how to survive in good circumstances, dangerous episodes, and times when nothing seems to go as planned.

Today, we often hear David described as a man after God's own heart, instantly bringing to mind the Michelangelo image. But looking closer, we see David poured himself out so that we might have a glimpse into what it takes to be *one after God's own heart.*

As a boy, David overcame the giant Goliath, but as an adult, and later as king of Israel, he faced many giant-sized challenges. His life was full of adventurous escapes and episodes that can teach and inspire us to overcome visible and invisible giants we face as we go through our later years.

—*Expect God to do the Unexpected*—

Are there events from earlier years that made such impact that you still carry them with you today? For most of us, there were moments in our early years that were turning points, defining moments. These are moments God continues to use in our lives.

David's story rings with some of the same similarity. Something unexpected was about to happen that would change things. Samuel, a prophet, was sent to Bethlehem, to the house of Jesse, to find a new king for Israel. All of Jesse's sons were impressive, but it was his youngest son, David, the one looking after the sheep, whom God told Samuel to anoint as the new king.

Meanwhile the Philistines were gathering their troops, preparing to wage war. They had state-of-the-art resources, equipped in every way to completely overwhelm any enemy they might face. All that, and a giant warrior.

Goliath challenged the Hebrew army. At three cubits, he was roughly nine feet tall and confident he would win.

Then there was David, sent by his father to carry food to his brothers who were serving in the army. He saw and heard firsthand the challenge Goliath had put

> *As we see with David, vulnerability requires a step back, to seek a new tool from our tool belts.*

forth. David had no training to do battle; he'd been trained to tend and protect sheep. Yet his young heart was horrified that the Philistine giant had taken charge, so David decided to step up and battle Goliath.

When we are vulnerable, we need to step back and seek a different tool from our tool belts. So what did David have as a weapon? A slingshot. But David was quite good with it. The responsibility his father assigned to him while his older brothers fought in Saul's army had been to tend sheep and keep other animals away. He had developed expertise in using the slingshot to tend the flock. But David was, after all, little more than a teenager. He'd never fought with a sword in his life.

David sized up the situation. Embarrassed that the giant Goliath had made cowards of the Hebrew army, he decided to do something about it. He collected *five smooth stones*, like the ones he often placed in his slingshot to protect his sheep, and prepared himself to do battle.

King Saul put his own armor on the shepherd boy. It wasn't a perfect fit for David, but the image of armor was very powerful. Goliath's physique was engulfed in his own armor, the picture of strength and stature. But even those who exude this kind of image have vulnerabilities, and David put one smooth stone in his sling and went out to find the giant's weakness.

Goliath was full of himself, making fun of what he was seeing. But suddenly the shepherd boy swung his

> *David was not only the hero, but he eventually became king.*

sling until it gained its full speed and power. He let the stone fly, and it struck Goliath's forehead. The great giant fell. The Philistine army fled. Goliath, fresh from jostling his enemies with laughter and contempt, was no more.

Eugene Peterson, author of *The Message*, calls the story of David and Goliath the greatest story ever told, for children and adults as well. David isn't the one most likely to succeed in this story. He's not the one with the most physical prowess. He isn't a trained fighter, but he had been equipped by God to defeat the enemy.

We may already find we have something in common with David. We may see ourselves as weaker, less capable, and often ill equipped. Let's face it: even if we are aging normally, our minds and bodies are not what they used to be.

David chose *five* smooth stones from the river to overcome the giant. He only needed *one*, but he had all five ready. Let's pretend that we, like David, have five smooth stones, five approaches to navigate life's journey in our later years. These five smooth stones will help us to overcome the challenges that can become fearful giants if we let them:

First Smooth Stone	• Understanding
Second Smooth Stone	• Seeing Things Differently
Third Smooth Stone	• Believing and Trusting
Fourth Smooth Stone	• Embracing
Fifth Smooth Stone	• Praying (Puts Us on Target)

The First Smooth Stone: *Understanding*

Over the last few decades, a gradual yet steady shift has been occurring. No longer are our later years the rocking-chair retirement of the past. Staying engaged, no matter how one does it, is highly encouraged. So much so that one doesn't have to look far for life-long learning opportunities.

Some may choose the high-adventure route, building an over-the-top bucket list. But this smooth stone isn't about tackling high adventure. It's about remaining in this adventure we call life, continuing to learn and understand the lessons of our experiences and challenges.

> *Things began to turn in favor of Jewish victories when David and Goliath met on the battlefield that day. But it was David's ability to embrace and understand the situation that allowed them to win the day.*

If we're thinking about it, wrapping our faith around it, then insight may follow. It's as St. Francis of Assisi writes of his desire to be understood, as well as to understand.

What we must face in our later years are new situations that may be larger than we are. We've never been in that exact situation before. We don't exactly know what to do. Let David's ability to understand the situation be our coach, our illustration. Like David, take the issue to the Lord. Ask the question, "What is the key to handling my problem?" David prayed in Psalm 32:7, NIV: "You are my hiding place; you will protect me from trouble and surround me with songs of deliverance."

Then comes the answer from the Lord: "I will instruct you and teach you in the way you should go; I will counsel you with my loving eye."

Be patient and listen with the ears of your soul. The answer will come.

The Second Smooth Stone: *Seeing Things Differently*

Have you ever thought about how much we're bound by how we see things? When David faced Goliath on that momentous day, there were three distinct ways folks looked at the very same scene.

1. Goliath and the Philistines looked at David and saw a runt. Goliath laughed, scorned, and belittled him. There are always those who want to make themselves look big by making others look small. It didn't work for Goliath, and it doesn't work for people today either. Goliath couldn't see what was *really* happening.

2. The Israelite army saw a mismatch, a debacle, and they were ready to run. They saw a giant and a boy, and were terrified for the boy and themselves. Some probably felt guilty for letting the kid do what they should have been doing.

3. What David saw was straightforward: *he simply saw an exposed forehead.*

When we face a huge Goliath-type circumstance in our lives, our first response is to be overwhelmed. But we need to find what we've overlooked. Don't let the giants steal your joy. David

> *The basic principal of faith: When things look bleak, look again, and again, and again. Try to see things in a different way.*

saw what everyone else overlooked, and he went for it.

A thousand years later in New Testament times, Paul was a master at looking at things again and again. To his Corinthian brothers and sisters in Christ, he revealed he had been given a "thorn in the flesh." It was, he said, a messenger of Satan sent to harass him.

A pharmacist at a local drugstore asked a pastor friend, "What do you think was Paul's thorn in the flesh?"

The pastor replied, "I don't know, but I think it was probably his eyesight or possibly a good case of malaria."

> *Our later years can cause us to get caught up in our giant-sized worries, but we must see them in a different way.*

Paul prayed about his thorn in the flesh three times and asked God to take it from him. God didn't remove it from him but showed him that he needed to see it differently. He needed to see his thorn in a completely different way.

> **Not as an enemy but as a blessing;**
> **Not as a foe but a friend;**
> **Not as a weakness but a strength.**

When he saw things differently, nothing changed for Paul on the outside, but everything changed on the inside. He started to see his weakness as a real strength. As the Lord put it, "My grace is sufficient for you, for power is made perfect in weakness" (2 Corinthians 12:9).

When you face your own giant, keep looking at the situation until you can see it in a new way. "So David triumphed over the Philistine with a sling and a stone … there was no sword in his hand" (1 Samuel 17:50).

Do you not often face circumstances that are bigger than you are?

- You're told by the doctor, "We need to do a biopsy to see if it's malignant."
- A spouse needs full-time care.
- The doctor says you can't live alone anymore.
- You realize you can't do all the things you used to enjoy … with either your body or your mind.
- Your circle is shrinking, as many friends and family are no longer with you.
- Relationships are strained or broken.

You and God can handle any circumstance together if you will let the Lord show you a better, and certainly a different, way to look at it.

The Third Smooth Stone: *Believing and Trusting*

David, unlike many of his contemporaries, was a believer. He believed not only in the power of God, but in himself.

Goliath treated young David like an annoying mosquito buzzing around his head. David's reply: "You come against me with sword and spear and javelin; but I come to you in the name of the Lord of Hosts, the God of the armies of Israel, whom you have defied" (1 Samuel 17:45).

David couldn't have done what he did without God. But God could not have done what needed to be done without David. Not only did David believe in God, but God also believed in David.

> *David believed God could do the impossible in unexpected ways. David believed in a partnership between him and God.*

We often talk and think about becoming believers in matters of faith. Usually we're referencing what we think, what we've analyzed, and our own belief systems. But believing is more than embracing a set of intellectual doctrines, although that may be important. *Believing involves trust.* It's trusting that you and God can become partners. You need God's power and wisdom. He needs your skills and gifts. God, you see, could not have done what He did without David's skill with that sling. God needed David's courage, needed his vision, and eventually needed his Psalms, over seventy of which still survive in our Old Testament.

Embrace two essential truths: David without God is nowhere. But God needs David's sling and those stones from the brook. In a similar way, God needs us and the understanding we have as we confront our own giants.

> *Anything that gets between each one of us and our relationship with Christ is a Goliath.*

Psalm 37 reflects David's thoughts about believing and trusting.

> Do not fret because of the wicked; do
>
> not be envious of wrongdoers,
>
> For they will soon fade like the grass,
>
> and whither like the green herb.
>
> Trust in the Lord, and do good; so you will
>
> live in the land, and enjoy security.
>
> Take delight in the Lord, and he will give
>
> you the desires of your heart.
>
> Commit your way to the Lord; trust
>
> in him, and he will act.

(Psalm 37:1–5)

Trust God to be your amour as you face your own goliath battles.

The Fourth Smooth Stone: *Embracing*

The Bible uses the word *redemption* to describe what David and Jesus did. A beautiful example of what *redemption* means is found in 2 Samuel, chapter 9. It's about Mephibosheth, the son of Jonathan (David's best friend) and the grandson of King Saul.

Life was not kind to Mephibosheth. He almost never got to see his father or grandfather. They were always out fighting the Philistines. That meant he, in essence, lost his childhood. It's hard to play on the swing when the enemy is burning the crops in the next field. War has never been kind to anyone, especially children.

One day the Philistines came, recklessly burning everything in sight. Mephibosheth's nurse grabbed him to run for cover. She tripped, and the boy broke both ankles, which left him permanently crippled.

The final blow for Mephibosheth came when his father, Jonathan, and his grandfather, Saul, were killed in the battle of Gilboa. Mephibosheth was without family. He was alone. In those days, people who were physically unable to function "normally" were discarded, especially if they had no family. So after the deaths of Saul and Jonathan, the question was, "What do we do with Mephibosheth?" Given the culture and time, a crippled person might as well have been paralyzed. Their options were limited. David was advised to get rid of Mephibosheth.

But David had a choice, just like Jesus did when a blind man named Bartemaeus called out, "Jesus ... have mercy on me."

Jesus said, "Come" (Mark 10:46–49).

David said to Mephibosheth, "[You] shall always eat at my table" (2 Samuel 9:7, 10).

There may be a thing or two that is crippling you, things that you carry in the back of your mind. You may have been praying about them for years, and nothing has been resolved. Truth is, they

> *The Lord Jesus has saved us, including saving us from those things that cripple us.*

won't likely be redeemed in your lifetime. But that doesn't impede the Lord Jesus from coming to you and saying, "Come sit at my table." Some think God is in the business of perfection. They think God goes around with a microscope, like Sherlock Holmes, looking for flaws. And when He finds them, He scowls and throws lightning bolts.

But the Gospel doesn't say that God is the inspector general of the universe. *The Gospel speaks of redemption.* What is redemption? The Bible states that redemption is the serious business of heaven.

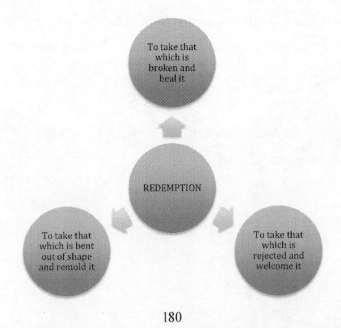

If you're God, knowing what's going on is no big deal. *Putting things back together without overriding human choice, that is a big deal indeed.* It is called *redemption.* It cost our Lord Jesus a cross—a crown of thorns. As one theologian Jurgen Moltmann puts it, redemption means a crucified God.

Eugene Peterson, author of *The Message*, has a unique and wonderful translation of Psalm 36, which paints in contemporary phrases the beauty and power of our redemption by God's amazing grace. Here are verses 5–8:

> God's love is meteoric, his love astronomic,
> His purpose titanic, his verdicts oceanic.
> Yet in his largeness nothing gets lost;
> Not a man, not a mouse, slips through the cracks.
> How exquisite your love, O God!
> How eager we are to run under your wings.
> To eat our fill at the banquet you spread
> As you fill our tankards with Eden spring water.

If grace begins with God's unlimited acceptance, it ends with redemption.

The Fifth Smooth Stone: *Praying Puts Us on Target*

David prayed about everything. Almost half of the psalms in the Old Testament, over seventy, were prayed and written down by David. What a great gift. After all, these are prayers that were written roughly three thousand years ago. These psalms speak, sustain, and encourage us. Sometimes they even correct us as they corrected David.

David wasn't a perfect man. In fact, he was flawed in some gigantic ways. But if his psalms are any example, he was honest when he exposed himself to God. No pretense. Sometimes he was at his best—and he prayed about it. Sometimes he was at his worst—and he prayed about that too.

—In All Circumstances—

The smooth stone analogy works well for us in our later years. In fact, we realize we created a toolkit years ago: where we go with life's challenges, how we respond, when we pull the worn, tattered drawstring bag out of our pockets and pull one (or more) stones out. Truth is, if we allow Him, the Lord will hand us the smooth stone we need when we need it. David shows us that prayer is the capstone.

Three psalms, side by side, emphasize how David prayed about everything: Psalm 22, Psalm 23, and Psalm 24.

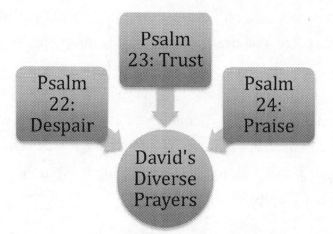

Psalm 22 finds David praying when he's deeply distressed, even depressed. An expression of despair is in the first verse: "My God, My God, why have you forsaken me?" These are words Jesus quoted from the cross. At the beginning of his prayer, David feels forsaken and abandoned, even by God. Verse 6 is an agonizing expression after others have rejected him: "I am a worm and not human; scorned by others and despised by the people. All who see me mock at me; they make mouths at me and shake their heads." But in the middle of the prayer (verses 19–22), he turns from his despair to his petition: "But you, O Lord, do not be far away; O my help, come quickly to my aid … I will tell of your name to my brothers and sisters; in the midst of the congregation I will praise you."

Psalm 23 begins and ends with a trusting, confident, believing thrust:

The Lord is my shepherd, I shall not want. He makes me lie down in green pastures; he leads me beside still waters;

he restores my soul. He leads me in the right paths for his namesake. Yea even though I walk through the darkest valley, I fear no evil; for you are with me; your rod and staff—they comfort me. You prepare a table before me in the presence of my enemies; you anoint my head with oil; my cup overflows. Surely goodness and mercy shall follow me all the days of my life, and I shall dwell in the house of the Lord my whole life long.

It has served as an encouraging whisper in the souls of believers through the centuries as they sought to find a way through difficult times.

Psalm 24, by contrast, is an *outburst of praise* for the greatness of the Lord: "The earth is the Lord's and everything in it, the world, and all who live in it; for he has founded it on the seas, and established it on the rivers." Then David, in his meditation, realizes the qualifications of those who can stand in the presence of God: "Those who have clean hands and pure hearts, who do not lift up their souls to what is false, and do not swear deceitfully. They will receive blessing from the Lord, and vindication from the God of their salvation."

How different are these three psalms, which stand back to back in the Psalter. Psalm 23 is an unforgettable testimony of trust and affirmation. Psalm 22 begins in total despair but keeps praying until a sense of spiritual strength returns. Psalm 24 reflects a heart lifted up in praise for the wonder of God's creation and a personal insight into spiritual growth and praise.

What we can learn from David's psalms is that we can pray about anything, in any mood, and while surrounded by any situation or circumstance.

Look at it this way: God already knows our situation, our mood, our joy, our despair. We've all

> *Prayer is the active side of God's grace.*

experienced that on the human scene. Sharing often makes a huge difference in a human relationship. How much more with God!

An incredible feature of David's prayers is usually overlooked … *David wrote his prayers down!* If he didn't, somebody did. It was probably both. David wrote down many of his prayers, whereas others may have written down the prayers David prayed with and for others. In either case, three thousand years later, we have them at our disposal to use as our own prayers or to learn from as we pray.

Writing down your prayers is a wonderful discipline. Just get an ordinary notebook, use a new page each day, and start. Write down whatever and whoever enters your mind as needing your prayers. Turn to your own needs and pray about them as you write them down. Pray through your day and write down what you pray about. It's encouraging to notice how many prayers have been answered when you look back over your prayed-for responsibilities at the end of the day or week.

Writing down prayers does several positive things. Prayers put in writing:

- Make you write down what you're really feeling and needing to share with God.
- Keep your mind on your praying. Your mind tends to wander.
- Preserve the expressions of your heart and mind for the future. When you read them again in the future you may gain insight or even encouragement from them.

David discovered that he had what he needed to face Goliath-sized challenges. With God's help, we can use our five smooth stones to face the challenges of our later years.

CHAPTER 12

The Adam Discovery:
Never Stop Starting

*The LORD God took the man and put him in
the Garden of Eden to work it and keep it.*
—Genesis 2:15 ESV

The Adam Discovery

Never Stop Starting

In 2007, at a busy Washington, DC, metro station, a young man with a baseball cap found an appropriate place to stand, watched as people passed by, and then took out his violin from its case and proceeded to play classical masterpieces, including Schubert's beloved "Ave Maria" and some of Bach's famous works.

Nearly three minutes of energetic playing passed before anyone took notice—a middle-aged man glanced over at the musician and then moved on. One woman noticed but merely threw a dollar in the musician's violin case as she hurried past. A few minutes later, a three-year-old boy wanted to stop, but his mother, pressed for time, hurried him along.

For nearly forty-five minutes, during which the musician played continuously, only seven people out of approximately eleven hundred who rushed past actually stopped and listened for a short while. About thirty gave money. The man collected a total of $32.17—pennies included. Each time the musician stopped, the sounds of ordinary hustle and bustle again took over. No one applauded.

No one knew it was violinist Joshua Bell, one of the greatest violinists in the world. The violin on which

> *What are we missing as we rush through life?*

he played at the metro was worth $3.5 million! Three days before, Bell's appearance had sold out a Boston theater where patrons shelled out one hundred dollars for mid-level seats, fans who went to great lengths to hear him play the same music as those passing unaware through the subway station.

This story, written by Pulitzer Prize winning journalist Gene Weingarten, was part of a social experiment by *The Washington Post* about perception, taste, and people's priorities, with its conclusion being, *"If we can't take the time out of our lives to stay a moment and listen to one of the best musicians on Earth playing some of the best music ever written ... then what else are we missing"* as we rush through daily life?[1] In our later years, we are beginning to sense a finiteness to our lives, and we recall the words those who have gone before always used to say: "Enjoy your youth; it goes by fast." For us it's, "Enjoy your final third, it goes by so fast." So in a way, we're rushed. Our chronological clocks are ticking.

When we read the Bible, too often we rush like those heading to work at the Metro Station. We're apt to miss the beautiful music. Worse, it is easy for us to miss the reality that this is not only the story of biblical characters but ours as well.

—Take Notice!—

Be observant. Notice the world around you. Become what I call "a noticer." Imagine yourself looking from an imaginary platform built on the tallest tree in the garden of Eden, a platform built so you can see in all directions—past, present, and future—enabling you to be a true noticer.

Note that the first three chapters of the Bible capture the difficulty and the wonder of creation. The authors—perhaps Moses was one of them—lived

> *The first three chapters of the Bible capture both the difficulty and the wonder of creation.*

before educational processes came into being, before language had extensive vocabularies, before science and astrophysics described the universe. Yet, through the Holy Spirit, the authors wrote their stories and have been our spiritual teachers through the centuries.

What we're apt to miss when we open the Bible and rush through the early verses is the beauty and the contrast they present. The Genesis picture begins with a beautiful description of God's new beginning: "God created the heavens and the earth" (Genesis 1:1). At this point we would expect a magnificent something, like a drum roll or Beethoven's "Symphony No. 5," which would lead us to the phenomenal picture of creation in its earlier moments.

But look again. There's no drum roll, no Beethoven's Fifth. Just the opposite:

> "The earth was a formless void and darkness covered the face of the deep." (Genesis 1:2)

In Genesis 1, Eden isn't there yet. There's no beauty in the description of God's new beginning. The beginning is without form. It's empty. Instead of light, there's darkness. While this is a description of how the universe actually began, it can also serve as a description of the new beginnings we enter in our lives, at any stage.

—Notice that Beginnings Can Be Hard—

Notice how God's new beginnings resemble our lives. Our later years are not as barren as the early description in Genesis. But if we expect new beginnings to immediately take the form and beauty of Eden, we'll be sorely disappointed. If Eden didn't appear at once for God's new beginnings, it won't for ours. We have to take the formlessness as a blank canvas, perhaps hum the tune until we begin to hear the music or see the color.

Beginnings can be difficult. It's true throughout life. Picture a little child learning to walk. It's trial and error, up and down, and little falls along the way. Now picture that same child in the many challenges of growing up, whether it's the first day of school, learning to read, learning to catch a ball, or playing the piano.

Any stage of adulthood has its challenges and new beginnings. Put the word *new* in front of any change in our lives. Challenges abound: a new job, new neighborhood, new marriage, or new responsibilities. When we pass through a new beginning as a child, there is usually someone near to coach us, to instruct us, to encourage us. But when we enter the final third of life, we may find ourselves mostly alone, without encouragement or direction.

This alone-ness can come upon us with jarring speed. One day we are part of a couple; then we are not. I recall speaking with a resident of a retirement center who had been through this very process. She had already entered later life, and she had significant health challenges, but her husband was with her and caring for her at home. Then, in the blink of an eye, it seemed, he was gone. The change was instantaneous and staggering.

For the first time in what seemed forever, she was living alone. Given her health needs, her children said, "Mom, you need to be in a place where you can receive the very best care." She stalled for a long time. Then she began to visit various places. Finally she made the decision. She moved to a retirement community after living in her home for almost fifty years. But, she told me, *moving was so hard*. She had to downsize, give away some furniture and several items she had cherished throughout her life. When the moving truck drove away with the things she would probably never see again, she wept. In that moment, she was discovering that some beginnings may be many things— exciting, challenging, emotional—but at the doorstep of the transition, it was hard.

—Nothing is Instantaneous—

Notice in Genesis, beginnings happen in stages. That's true when one is born and begins to grow up. It is still true as we're in the middle and later years of our life. Be patient with yourself. The earliest picture we have of God creating is one of gradual stages. Nothing happens instantly. Genesis divides the process of creation into six separate days. Eden isn't there yet.

The Hebrew word *day* in these early Genesis verses refers to a period of time, not necessarily a 24-hour day. We use the word in the same way. We might say, "In the day when there were not automobiles ..." We would be talking about a period of time, not a single dawn-to-dusk happening.

The picture the Bible is sketching for anyone making a new start is that nothing happens instantly.

> *Beginnings happen in stages. Nothing happens instantly.*

Be patient. God was not attached to anything that bore the label *instant*.

In Genesis 1, everything that happened by divine creation took time. By God's design, creating newness is a process, not a snap of the fingers.

In our later years, with all of its adjustments, arrangements, and changes, we do well to remember Genesis 1. As with the world's creation, adjusting to newness doesn't happen all at once but in stages. But if we're patient, what seems barren now eventually brings new beauty and growth, like Eden—barren newness will change to fruitful Eden, igniting possibilities.

—Notice that Rest Is Important—

With the pace of life, often something must be sacrificed. For many of us, demands on our time are still frenetic, and rest is

> *"The seventh day God finished the work . . . and he rested"*
> —Genesis 2:2

the only available option. It's no accident that we see a strong pattern of rest in the Scriptures.

The Hebrew word *Sabbath* means rest. The seventh day in our weekly calendar is often called the Sabbath. Its roots are in the earliest parts of the Bible. After six days of heavy creating, God rested. So when we set aside the seventh day for worship and rest, we are following the Creator. From the beginning, rest was crucial. Don't rush, make rest part of your new pattern. Secular society ignores such wisdom, but it is no accident God sets the example from the start.

God wants us to get our attention right at creation's door. Notice that one of the earliest pictures we have of God, the creator, demonstrates the importance of rest. Any time you have to make a major change in your life, schedule some times for rest and renewal. Jesus once said to His work-weary disciples, "Come away ... and rest for a while" (Mark 6:31). Even Jesus and His disciples needed times apart from responsibility and service. When you make a major change in your life, copy God, who rested after His heavy creating. You should become comfortable with resting as part of the process.

> *God sets the example. Don't rush; make rest part of your pattern.*

—*Relationships are a Crucial Part of Creation*—

When we are rested and restored, we are most ready to relate to those closest to us. We were created for relationships, for one another. Perhaps there is no greater human need than to have a sense of connection. What's often missed is that *Eden was created to be a relational place.* Many of our images of the garden are of Eden's beauty. But the beauty of relationship is also what God wants us to see and seek. In the words of James Weldon Johnson, God says, "I'm lonely. I think I'll make me a world."[2]

God creates Adam and Eve because He wants a personal relationship with His creation. For God, relationships are always at the foundation. Adam begins his life in relationship with God. Genesis 1:26 gives us the profound statement that God will make humans in His image; this may mean we're relational beings. We're not made to be loners. We are meant to be connected—to have friends and family and to understand God wants to be part of our family. So God created Eden where relationships could develop.

Genesis 2:15 describes the beginning of a key relationship: "The Lord God took the man and put him in the garden of Eden to till it and keep it." For Adam, this beginning had to be difficult. Think about it. He had no "How To" book. There were no traditions, no parents or grandparents or aunts and uncles or neighbors to ask questions. There were no rules, regulations, or policies. If he made a mistake, there was no Social Security to back him up. *Adam was the pioneer of beginnings.*

Genesis 2:15 offers us a picture of our lives! Like the garden of Eden, our lives must be tended. Others may help us. Others may be healers, or encouragers, or teachers. But in the end, we are to join with God in being responsible for the garden we call the self. *Shift your attention from Eden as Adam's place to Eden as your place and mine.* In our lives, the garden of Eden is *in* us, and we're responsible for tending it and caring for it. As Adam tended to Eden, so must we tend to the gardens of ourselves.

> *Then God said, "Let us make humankind in our image, in our likeness, and let them have dominion over the fish of the sea, and over the birds of the air, and over the cattle, and over all . . . [things] upon the earth."*
>
> —Genesis 1:26

The purpose of creation is not for God to look out from a celestial window and say, "Wow, look what I did." Oh no. God wants a relationship, a sharing partnership, with the persons He has created. The first relationship in Genesis is not between Adam and Eve, but between Adam and God. It's quite a picture. Just the two of them, Adam and God.

Our new beginnings are just like God's in early Genesis. We need to copy God. His pattern is to never stop starting. God could have washed his hands of the whole mess but He chose to begin again.

—God's Pattern: Never Stop Starting—

Jesus once told a parable about three men who were given talents and were instructed to put them to use and increase them. Two did and were commended and blessed with even more talents. But one, out of fear, hid his in the ground. Instead of a commendation for being careful and safe, he was given the condemning label of evil. To be sure, a talent in those days was a weight measurement, like an ounce or a pound. Its value was dependent upon whether gold or silver or copper was being measured. But the teaching of Jesus was clear. What you've been given is to be put to use. If you don't use it, you lose it. Jesus doesn't put age limits on life lessons.

Having a purpose for being alive is God's design for all of us. For Adam, it was "tend the garden and take care of it." That can become

> *The divine purpose for our lives is to take care of ourselves as Adam took care of Eden.*

a symbol, a picture, and what defines our story.

This is especially crucial in our later years when the self, called Eden, begins to age. The divine purpose for our lives is to take care of ourselves as Adam took care of Eden. Isn't there some wisdom for us there—never stop starting!

Years ago, a friend in his eighties, Shaw Cunningham, loved to garden. On occasion he would take people into his garden and show off something that had just come up or was in full bloom. His favorite saying was on a motto in his garden:

> *The kiss of the sun for pardon,*
> *The song of the birds for mirth,—*
> *One is closer to God in a garden*
> *Than anywhere else on earth.*[3]

Whether you agree with this motto about earthy gardening or not, this much is true: we must tend the garden of the personal Eden that is within us.

It's a remarkable notion: Eden within us. Our lives are like a spiritual garden that's to be cared for, tended, and cultivated. In early years, your parents may have tried to nurture this spiritual garden within. In middle

> *Here is the bold truth about our spiritual lives: I am the spiritual gardener of my own soul.*

age, our roles and responsibilities often dictated the landscape of our personal gardens. At this stage of our lives, our final third, no one else will define it or do it for us. We have the freedom to listen and notice God's voice in the garden. Some things have to be planted. Some things need to be uprooted and thrown away. Some relational and spiritual parts of us need to be cultivated, watered, encouraged, and affirmed. They need to be tended. Here's the foundational truth about our spiritual lives: I am the spiritual gardener of my own soul.

Will you consider that you are in *the best stage of your life* with the freedom to tend your spiritual garden? If so, you've now shifted the focus to noticing advantages of being older. For instance, if you're in your retirement years, you may have more discretionary time available than in previous years, and you can choose how to spend it.

—Notice That You Are Your Own Eden—

Whatever age we are, we're our own Eden. We have to become for ourselves what we've always been for others. We are now responsible to tend the garden called ourselves. It's our garden.

As we pause to look at ourselves in that garden mirror, we begin to realize that there are many plants, many parts of us that make up the Eden of the self. They need looking after. They need tending. Some are more easily cared for than others. These differ from person to person. But the bottom line is this: if we don't look after the gardens that make up ourselves, they deteriorate, they languish, they grow weeds, and they begin to show neglect.

A temptation for those who pass from one stage of life to another is to just quit doing the things we most enjoyed or to neglect the abilities that set us apart. We quit cultivating the gift God has given us, quit developing and expanding our talents and abilities. Those talents may not be what they once were, of course. We may find ourselves facing real limitations, physical or otherwise, which make it impossible to do things the way we once did. But don't miss that there's more than one way to go about it, and *growing into a new way of doing things may be what's needed.*

—Freedom—

> *In order to tend your Eden, you have to continue using, learning, and developing the gifts God has given you.*

Now the Genesis account takes a new turn. It records that God decided to make us in His image. *How can God make us in His image?* God's likeness becomes ours when we're given the *awesome gift of the freedom to choose.* In the graphic picture of the Genesis account, Adam and Eve are in the garden. God interrupts everything by giving them a choice: "Adam and Eve, come here a minute. Eat happily of the fruit of every tree in sight except one. Leave that one alone." The serpent comes. They give in. They eat. They're cast out of the garden of innocence.

Choice, to be real, must contain both a yes and a no. Consequences result from the choices we make. The truth is, you have made many, many choices already today, including getting out of bed, what you had for breakfast, and what did with your day.

> *Choices matter. Choices make us like God, but they also dictate what will happen.*

What we may not appreciate is that God makes us different from all of the rest of creation. With choices, we are given both a *yes* and a *no,* a *do* and a *don't.*

Choice is a distinctly human trait. For instance, it's well known that birds annually migrate from South America to North America at predictable times. Their calendar and flight patterns are passed on from generation to generation. In some cases, they never vary. The swallows return to Capistrano every year right on schedule, which brings tourists from all over. It never happens that the bird in the leadership position says, "Hey, let's change things up. Instead of spending the winter in Capistrano, let's go to the Bahamas this year." Birds don't have that choice.

Humans are different. When God created Adam and Eve, a new kind of being was created—someone who, in spite of difficulties, could choose to begin or not to begin, to change or not to change. In the case of Adam and Eve, the wrong choice was made. They were cast out of the garden of innocence and had to live with the consequences.

What is the recipe for tending the garden of the self?

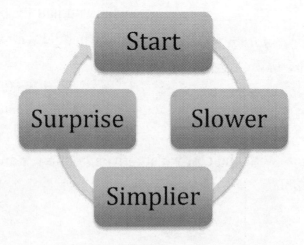

Start

In the second chapter of Genesis, we're given a picture of God's pattern to *never stop starting*. As with the very beginning of creation, God starts all over again with us. Most of the time, God simply starts with what He has to work with: us. He could've given up on Adam and Eve right there in the garden. Instead He never stops starting. He hopes we'll do the same in our relationship with Him and in our lives—right up until the end. Don't miss this incredible sketch of God, which happens at the very beginning of the Bible. While we have a God whose creation happened in stages, we also have a God who never stops creating new beginnings.

You may say, "But Genesis happened a long time ago." Yes, it did, but look at

> *God will never stop starting.*

Revelation. Another visionary, probably John the Apostle, sees through to the end of time and, lo and behold, God is still at it. Revelation 21:1: "Then I saw a new heaven and a new earth; for the first heaven and the first earth passed away." At the end of time as we know it, God will still be creating.

Slower

It's true researchers have found those of us at a certain age need more time to learn new things. The truth is, we need more time to do just about everything, not just new learning! So as we grow older, if we can accept our slower pace—quality versus quantity—speed is not a factor. We can prioritize and take care of what really matters. Then we may see what researchers have also found: we humans are doggedly diligent and especially capable once we're a little more seasoned in life.

Simpler

In earlier life stages, we had a long list of goals and plans for our lives, even a long to-do list for each day. Simplifying things is an important part of the journey, which signals that we acknowledge and accept our limitations. In later life, less is definitely more.

Surprise

Regardless of what has happened to you, please believe this truth: God isn't

> *Acknowledge and accept your limitations*

finished with you yet! Expect Him to surprise you. If you look closely, you'll probably notice that He's already delivered on this one. Something that you never dreamed you'd do, you're doing. Something you've waited years for actually happened. Surprise!

Before we leave this final lesson—never stop starting!—let me leave you with a passage I wrote in one of my earlier books, *God and Creation*. Written before I had reached the stage of later life, this passage encompassed my understanding of our lives and our relationship with God in the 1980s. Now that I *have* reached later life, I see my own earlier writings in a whole new light. And guess what? I believe in this passage now more than ever! I offer it again here for all of us who are now facing the challenges and opportunities of later life:

> Our beginnings are wrapped in the purposes of God at creation ... Our roots are earth-planted, but they are also God-planted. Terms like *new birth*, *conversion*, and *born again* testify to the eternal calling within man to find his roots in eternity and in God. These terms are not simply religious phrases, *churchy* words. They are reflections of a reality that exists beyond the chemical components that make up a human being. They speak to the inner and spiritual rootedness of man in God.[4]

Conclusion

Never Stop Starting

We humans are much better with beginnings than endings. We would rather hold a baby than visit a nursing home. We like daybreak better than midnight. Think of all of the books we begin to read but don't finish. We love to say hello; it's harder to say good-bye. And when you turn to John's Gospel, you really see this because his gospel begins crisp, precise, deep, and profound: "In the beginning was the Word, and the Word was with God, and the Word was God. Nothing came into being except through Him." When you get to the ending of John's Gospel, his crisp precision falters. It's as if John couldn't decide how to end. We get two endings!

Read chapter 20 and you will discover a piece of text that reads like a final chapter. It covers a period of time after the resurrection of Jesus Christ. It takes up the story after Jesus has been raised from the dead. In the early part of chapter 20, the disciples are cowering in fear, and then Jesus appears to Mary Magdalene and, later on, to the disciples. He breathes peace upon them and says to them, "As the Father has sent Me, I also send you" (John 20:21 NAS). Look at the last verse: "These are written that you may believe that Jesus is the Christ, the Son of God, and that by believing you may have life through his name." End of the Gospel, right?

Well, your eye catches something, and it says chapter 21, and the first word of chapter 21 is "Afterward." It's as if John adds chapter 21 as an afterthought. It's a bit like when we write a letter and we've finished it and addressed the envelope. We're folding the letter, and we are about to put it in an envelope, a stamp at the ready. Then we remember something else we needed to say. So we take the letter and write "p.s.—Oh, I forgot to mention ..." Have you ever done that?

If you were to read John 20 and 21 side by side, you'd think that John had an "Oh, I forgot to mention that" moment—which would become John 21. That is why many scholars say the Gospel of John has two endings. Maybe so; that would explain how chapter 21 got in there. John remembered an incredible day of fishing on the Sea of Galilee—and a very special breakfast with Jesus. And it's a good thing he remembered and added that postscript. The Lord has used John 21 to tell us a vitally important message. Hear it: *When God is present in an ending, there is always a new beginning.*

Let your mind's eye travel with me through the early verses of chapter 21. The resurrection has happened. Jesus has appeared twice to His disciples, but the appearances have been brief and they feel such loss. His physical presence isn't there anymore.

Did they imagine they saw Him? Did they dream it? What had really happened?

So they went home maybe to think it over, seven of them making the trek from Jerusalem back to the Sea of Galilee—not a short journey on foot. When they finally got there, Simon Peter—always impatient to get on with things—said, "I'm going fishing" (verse 3). The others went with him, not because it was their hobby, but because it had once been their living.

Three years earlier, when Jesus had called them as disciples, fishing was their business. Then came the day when Jesus walked by and said, "Your nets can wait; follow me." And they had followed him … until they did not know what to do and went back home. So they got in the boat that day, or really it would have been late afternoon, and the ones who took the oars got them away from the bank and into the deep where they could put up the sail. I imagine their thoughts were not on fishing. They were lost in thought over what had happened during the last three years—during the last incredible days, the crucifixion, and the appearances of the risen Lord.

Suppose you put yourself in their places. They get out in the middle of that large lake, the Sea of Galilee. Now these guys who have been away from it for three years, they don't pull out rods and reels. They fish with heavy nets, nets with seaweed and fish scales on them, and they pick those nets up together. In that time and place, fishing with nets was a togetherness thing, a carefully coordinated and cooperative effort. And do you know what? They hadn't lost the coordination of it at all. They picked up those old, heavy nets. They knew that the next morning their muscles would be a little grouchy, but they had the muscle memory that allowed them to do it.

But that night's fishing turned out to be a disaster. Time after time, they threw out the nets, and they caught absolutely nothing. One of them doubtless said, "You know, maybe everything has changed since we left, but I don't remember us ever being out here and not catching anything." And in the midst of their emptiness, empty of net and empty of heart, they heard a voice.

Or perhaps they thought they might have heard something. Imagine their mumbling in the boat as the dawn began to break. Did you hear that? Hear what? Never mind that, what are we going to do now? I heard something . . . well, I can't be sure. I'm tired. Not a single fish? That's impossible. Why did we come back here anyway? I guess I didn't hear anything.

At that point, the disciples were spiritually stuck. As the late Michael Yaconelli might have said, "They were stuck in their stuckness." They were stuck because they could not go back, but they saw no way forward. There was no sense going back to Jerusalem, because Jesus was no longer there to give them guidance. But their old way of life—their fishing—was practically mocking them. Stuck.[1]

If you find yourself in a state of "stuckness," you are going to need some stepping stones to get you out of the quagmire. And the first stepping stone is to listen for God's voice.

I can see Peter punching John and saying, "Did you hear anything? Did you hear that?" And from the shore, from a person they can't quite see clearly, they do hear the voice. *This is the first stepping stone: Listen to the voice that is within you.* It is the voice of God—that quiet prompting that comes to help you in your stuckness. When you need a new beginning, when you don't know the next step to take, when you feel too weary to press onward, be still and listen for God's voice in your heart of hearts.

Listen to the voice, because the voice that you hear is apt to be the spirit of God shuffling around in your soul. And the disciples in the boat did listen. It took them a while to understand, but eventually they heard the Lord saying, "Put your net on the other side of the boat—the right side of the boat." And they did. They had nothing to lose. All of a sudden the fish were everywhere, and the whole area around the boat was alive with fish. By listening to God's voice and then acting upon it, their night of emptiness was transformed into a morning of abundance.

Most of us have experienced this kind of transformation in some way or another during our lives, often in later life. Sue Monk Kidd, author of the beloved novel *The Secret Life of Bees*, wrote earlier in her career the story of a woman who had a difficult journey through the dark night of the soul and how God helped her transcend it: "It is as if God lifted the lid of a music box in a dark room inside of me and then vanished. It's a beautiful tune, a new sound and hearing it I can't forget, but I am like a child, leaving my nursery, stumbling through a dark house in search of the music maker."[2]

That's where the disciples were. They were in search of the music maker. The Lord Christ, who had made music in their lives, wasn't there anymore. Then they heard the voice. They heard, "Do something different. Put your net on the other side." And when John figured it all out, he cried, "It's the Lord!" (John 21:7).

Let me ask you something. In your heart and mind, are you in need of a new start? Do you feel stuck? Do you keep wondering what your next step should be? *You are not alone!* Others feel that way, too. Even the disciples felt that way. They felt that way *after* the resurrection of their Lord. If the disciples can feel stuck in that moment, then we need not feel ashamed when we feel stuck in more ordinary circumstances.

But here is the most important point about being stuck. You are not alone because *God is standing on your shore*. The Lord is at work and speaking to you in your heart of hearts. John's postscript, his second ending, makes this clear: It's the Lord, and He has something important to tell you.

Simon Peter, always the first to act, jumped out of the boat and swam to the shore. And, by the way, he left all the work for everybody else. On this occasion, they probably didn't mind much. Jesus was back! They gathered in the catch and hastened to shore.

That morning in Galilee, Jesus fixed a breakfast of fish and bread for the disciples. There is a subtle but important point in that. He served them a breakfast, which, for them, was perfectly normal: fish and bread. The breakfast food was normal, but the voice and presence of the risen Lord was not. God often works that way, conveying remarkable messages to our hearts in the most ordinary settings.

Breakfast in Galilee. It turned out to be not the celebration of an ending, but the announcement of a beginning. In this case, Jesus' closest followers were the unlikely bunch of beginners. He served them a basic meal, and he gave them a challenging new task. The spiritual life is like that. So often you come to a place where you are called to be a beginner—again!—and to start anew.

When breakfast was over, Jesus spoke directly to Peter. He said, "Peter, do you love me?" And Simon Peter said, "Lord, you know I love you."[3]

Now we might expect Jesus to say, "Then why in world did you betray me on the night I needed you the most?" Or He might have said, "If you love me, get on your knees and worship me." He didn't say anything about His crucifixion. Jesus didn't say anything about Himself.

213

He said, "Take care of my people." *Take care of my people!* He turned the whole focus on *somebody else* in need.

Three times, Jesus asked Peter the same question: "Do you love me?" Each time, Peter answers, "Of course I do, Lord!" And each time that Peter answers "yes," Jesus repeats Peter's new calling—a new calling for all of his followers, including us. Jesus offers Peter three "if-then" commands.

Jesus: Do you love me?

Peter: Yes, I love you, Lord!

Jesus: If so, then "feed my lambs" (verse 15); if so, then "tend my sheep" (verse 16); if so, then "feed my sheep" (verse 17).

Each task has to do with shepherding. It's about pouring out your love on behalf of somebody else. It's a mission that gets you outside of yourself.

That is another stepping stone for moving forward. If you are trying to put your life back together, and you feel stuck, think about what Jesus might suggest that you do. Think about what he told Peter. Tend my sheep. When you feel paralyzed by the challenges of later life, consider what Jesus might say to you: *You are never too old to love somebody in need.*

Who is it in your life that needs your love? What Jesus was saying to Peter, and to us, is simple: "Go find somebody who you can love, and, in loving them, you will make all of the difference." That love will give you a taste of the character of our Lord Jesus and the Holy Spirit. Yes, even in your later life. Perhaps especially so!

As a preacher, I've held the hands of many who have made their final journey home. Once, when the sudden, tragic loss of a dear one blindsided me, our organist saw my need, and in that moment of grief, he found a way to give comfort. He handed me a copy of Don Wyrtzen's well-known hymn, "Finally Home," whose lyrics comfort the heart and speak to us of new beginnings: "Just thinking of stepping on shore and finding it heaven / Of touching a hand and finding it God's / Of breathing new air and finding it celestial / Of waking up in Glory and finding it 'Home'."[4]

For we who remain, someone's death is an ending. But for every believer who goes home to be with the Lord, it's a beginning. Just think about waking up in glory and finding it home. What a comforting thought that is.

In the meantime, let's take comfort in the idea that our later years can be vital and fruitful. Just as Jesus called to his disciples from the shore of Galilee, God stands at the door of our hearts and knocks. He is waiting for us to hear him, waiting for our "yes." He has plans for our final third. Even as we lean upon Him for strength and courage, He seeks to use our experience and talents in new and unanticipated ways—to change the world around us in ways large and small.

Before that breakfast in Galilee, the disciples were at a complete loss. They had given their lives to a cause—to their Lord—and by witnessing His resurrection, they recognized that they were absolutely right to believe that Jesus was indeed the Messiah. But then the risen Lord was suddenly gone from them. This was the last thing they had expected, and, what was more, Jesus had vanished without giving them a plan, without a blueprint for their future.

Later life often hits us with the same suddenness—a lost spouse, a lost home, a lost purpose. In an instant, our lives change in ways we could not expect. Careful retirement plans go up in thin air. Financial security collapses. Good health goes bad. We find ourselves lost in uncharted waters. We are afraid, paralyzed with fear. We feel lonely. We find ourselves merely existing— not really living. This is not at all what we planned. We don't know what to do.

The disciples had tried to cope by doing what most of us would do when faced with sudden, bewildering change. They returned to what was familiar—in their case, fishing for a living. But trying to recapture what once was familiar to us seldom works out the way we hope it will. The disciples caught no fish at all.

Then, when all seemed lost, Jesus called to them. They had ears to hear, and they had open hearts. And what they received in return was a new purpose for their lives. Once more, they were beginners. Once more, they started again. Jesus taught them the lesson they most needed to hear: Never Stop Starting!

Starting again begins with your inner heart saying, "It's the Lord." It continues when you realize you can make a difference, and it takes another stride forward when you commit yourself to caring for someone who is in great need. Being willing to start again opens wonderful opportunities for your later life.

Rich and poor, exceptional and ordinary, powerful and outcast— the Biblical characters discussed in this book all found ways to make their later lives count. In doing so, they left us clues for finding vitality and purpose in the final stage of our own lives. This lesson is not merely for those facing the challenges of later life; it is also a universal dynamic for people of all ages. It applies to those of us moving through our later lives, and it applies equally well for our caregivers.

Please embrace this message from the Bible: Never Stop Starting! And then take one more step in faith. *Believe from the bottom of your heart that every ending in God's grace is a new beginning.*

Notes

Introduction

[1]   Peter James Flamming, *Healing the Heartbreak of Grief* (Nashville, TN: Abingdon Press, 2010).

[2]   Daniel J. Levinson, et al., *The Stages of a Man's Life* (New York: Ballantine Books, 1978); and idem., *The Seasons of a Woman's Life* (New York: Ballantine Books, 1996). Gail Sheehy, *Passages: Predictable Crises of Adult Life* (originally published 1976; 30th anniversary Edition, New York: Ballantine, 2006); and idem., *New Passages: Mapping Your Life Across Time* (New York: Random House, 1995). See also two books by Elizabeth MacKinlay: *The Spiritual Dimension of Aging* (London: Jessica Kingsley Publishers, 2001); and *Spiritual Growth and Care in the Fourth Age of Life* (London: Jessica Kingsley Publishers, 2006).

[3]   Robert S. Weiss and Scott A. Bass, *Challenges of the Third Age: Meaning and Purpose in Later Life* (Oxford and New York: Oxford University Press, 2002).

[4]   Richard Rohr, *Falling Upward: A Spirituality for the Two Halves of Life* (San Francisco, CA: Jossey-Bass, 2011).

Chapter 1: Moses

[1]   Sara Lawrence-Lightfoot, *The Third Chapter: Passion, Risk, and Adventure in the 25 Years after 50* (New York: Sarah Crichton Books, 2009), 30.

[2]   Richard J. Leider, *The Power of Purpose*, 2nd Edition (San Francisco, CA: Berrett-Koehler Publishers, 2010); see also Richard J. Leider and David A. Shapiro, *Repacking Your Bags: Lighten Your Load for the Good Life*, Third Edition (San Francisco, CA: Berrett-Koehler Publishers, 2012); and Leider

and David Shapiro, *Claiming Your Place at the Fire: Living the Second Half of Your Life on Purpose* (San Francisco, CA: Berrett-Koehler Publishers, 2004), ix–xv.

3   Robert Morris, "Looking for Meaning in a Life's Experience," in Robert S. Weiss and Scott A. Bass, *Challenges of the Third Age: Meaning and Purpose in Later Life* (New York: Oxford University Press, 2002), 161–172.

4   Harry Kollatz Jr. and Melissa Scott Sinclair, "The Heirloom-Makers," *Richmondmagazine.com*, April 1, 2010.

5   E. Craig McBean and Henry C. Simmons, *Thriving Beyond Midlife* (Institute for Integral Retirement Planning, 2006).

6   Alfred, Lord Tennyson, "Ulysses," originally published in 1842, is widely reprinted. An audio version is online at poetryfoundation.org.

7   Richard J. Leider and David A. Shapiro, *Claiming Your Place at the Fire: Living the Second Half of Your Life on Purpose* (San Francisco, CA: Berrett-Koehler Publishers, 2004), ix–xv.

Chapter 2: Barnabas

1   This story has found a wide circulation on the Internet (especially among pastors seeking a parable for a sermon or lecture), and the details of the story vary from site to site. Begin with Os Guinness' website: osguinness.com.

2   William Barclay, *The Letter to the Hebrews*, Revised edition (originally published 1955; Louisville, KY: Westminster John Knox Press, 1976), 122–123.

3   Diane Milnes, *Be an Encourager* (EnerPower Press, 2011).

4   Michael Yaconelli, *Messy Spirituality* (Grand Rapids, MI: Zondervan, 2007), 102.

5   Eric Butterfield, "Love: The One Creative Force," in Jack Canfield and Mark Victor Hansen, authors and compilers, *Chicken Soup for the Soul: 101 Stories to Open the Heart and Rekindle the Spirit* (Deerfield, FL: Health Communications Inc., 1993), 3–4.

6   The Bible does not explain Saul's name change to Paul and there are many interpretations, which need not concern us here. For the record, sections of the book of Acts, chapters 7-8, recount Saul's persecution of early believers; chapter 9 relates Saul's conversion and exile to Tarsus. Saul reappears in chapter 12, when Barnabas goes to Tarsus to bring him to Antioch. In chapter 13, Barnabas and Saul go to preach the gospel on Cyprus and in verse 9,

we first read: "Saul, who was also called Paul" (ESV). Thereafter, the New Testament uses the name Paul exclusively.

[7] Robert L. Cate, *One Untimely Born: The Life and Ministry of the Apostle Paul* (Macon, GA: Mercer University Press, 2006).

Chapter 3: Abraham

[1] Carlo Coretto, *The God Who Comes*, translated by Rose M. Hancock (New York: Corbis Books, 1974).

[2] Thomas Cahill, *The Gifts of the Jews* (New York: Nan A. Talese/Anchor Books, 1999), 63.

[3] Gregg Levoy, *Callings: Finding and Following an Authentic Life* (New York: Three Rivers Press, 1998), 9.

[4] Charles Colson, *Loving God* (Grand Rapids, MI: Zondervan, 1996), 24.

[5] The poem "The Tragedy of the Unopened Gift," part of which is used here, is often attributed to Gregg Levoy. But as Levoy confirmed via email exchange (October 2015), he himself did not write this poem; nor does he know how it came to be associated with him, although he has seen it attributed it to him on the Internet for years. Another Internet mystery! The poem used here is printed in John Ortberg, *If You Want to Walk on Water Get Out of the Boat* (Grand Rapids, MI: Zondervan, 2014), 35-36.

Chapter 4: Paul

[1] The survey was conducted by The Boomer Project (theboomerproject.com), a marketing agency, which surveyed nearly 900 "seniors" (age 63 and up) and over 1,600 caregivers (ages 35-62) in both the United States and Canada. The results are reprinted online via Home Instead Senior Care at two of their company's websites:
http://www.caregiverstress.com/fitness-nutrition/get-mom-moving/fears-about-aging/ and, http://www.homecareinphoenix.com/the-top-ten-fears-of-elderly-adults-2/

[2] Emilie Griffin, *Souls in Full Sail: A Christian Spirituality for Later Years* (Downers Grove, IL: InterVarsity Press, 2011), 11–12.

[3] Ibid., 75–79.

[4] Ibid., 82–83, 88.

[5] Simone Weil, *Waiting for God* (New York: HarperCollins, 2001).

6   Andrew H. Selle, "Face Down that Fear by Faith and Love! A Biblical and Transformative Model," available online at http://www.ccmvt.org/articles/fear_overcoming.pdf

7   Ruth Graham, with Stacy Mattingly, *A Legacy of Faith: Things I Learned from my Father* (Grand Rapids, MI: Zondervan, 2006). The quotations are at the end of chapter 1, but the entire chapter is a must read!

Chapter 5: Anna

1   Results reported in Harry R. Moody, "Introduction: Knowledge, Practice, and Hope," in Harry R. Moody, ed., *Religion, Spirituality, and Aging: A Social Work Perspective* (originally published 2008; New York: Routledge, 2010), 21. The quotes in the paragraphs that follow are from Susan Perschbacher Melia, "Solitude and Prayer in the Late Lives of Elder Catholic Women: Religious Activity, Withdrawl, or Transcendence?" *Journal of Religious Gerontology* (2002), vol. 13(1): 47-63.

2   Lydia K. Manning, Jessie A. Leek, and M. Elise Radina, "Making Sense of Extreme Longevity: Explorations into the Spiritual Lives of Centenarians" *Journal of Religion, Spirituality and Aging*, vol. 24, no. 4, (2012): 345–359.

Chapter 6: Esther

1   Francis Dorff, *The Art of Passing Over: An Invitation to Living Creatively* (Mesa, CA: Paulist Press, 1988).

2   Bronnie Ware, *The Top Five Regrets of Dying: A Life Transformed by the Dearly Departed* (London: Hay House, 2011). The list is reproduced online at: http://www.theguardian.com/lifeandstyle/2012/feb/01/top-five-regrets-of-the-dying

3   Elliot Dorff, *Matters of Life and Death: A Jewish Approach to Modern Medical Ethics* (Philadelphia, PA: The Jewish Publication Society, 1998).

4   "5 Good Things about Aging," *Consumer Health Reports*, vol. 25, no. 5 (May 2013).

Chapter 7: Joseph

1   Alan Stringfellow, *Great Characters of the Bible* (Tulsa, OK: Hensley Publishing, 1980), 35.

Chapter 8: Mary

[1] Nicholas Wolterstorff, *Lament for a Son* (Grand Rapids, MI: Wm. B. Eerdmans, 1987), 15.

[2] J. William Worden, *Grief Counseling and Grief Therapy: A Handbook for the Mental Health Practitioner*, Fourth Edition (New York: Springer Publishing Company, 2009).

[3] This section of the text, "Living with Grief," and, more broadly, this chapter on grief, is taken largely from my book, *Healing the Heartbreak of Grief* (Nashville, TN: Abingdon Press, 2010), a work based not only from many years in ministry, but also, in a far more personal way, from the loss of my son, Dave, to cancer. The "Three Rules" listed above are discussed in chapter 2, "What Do I Do Now?"

Chapter 9: John

[1] Alan Walker, *Franz Liszt: The Man and His Music* (Tapliger Publishing Company, 1970), 87.

[2] John Kendall, ed., *Extracts from the Writings of Francis (sic) [Francois] Fenelon, Archbishop of Cambray* (translated and published in English, 1804; Ulan Press, 2012), quotes from pp. 64–69.

Chapter 10: Naomi and Ruth

[1] My analysis of Naomi and Ruth in this chapter is based in part on my earlier book, *Healing the Heartbreak of Grief* (Nashville, TN: Abingdon Press, 2010), chapter 9.

[2] Marjory Zoet Bankson, Revised Edition, *Seasons of Friendship: Naomi and Ruth as Models for Relationship* (Minneapolis, MN: Augsburg Fortress Publishers, 2005), 46.

[3] Ibid., chapter 1.

[4] Richard Rohr, *Falling Upward*, 117.

[5] Jane Brody, "Forging Connections for a Longer Life," blog in the New York Times "Well" section, March 26, 2012. Access at: http://well.blogs.nytimes.com/2012/03/26/forging-social-connections-for-longer-life/

Brody is citing the first 2006 printing of Robbins' book. For the next year's reprint: John Robbins, *Healthy at 100: The Scientifically Proven Secrets of the World's Healthiest and Longest-Lived Peoples* (Ballantine Books; 1st Reprint edition, 2007).

6   Diane Barth, "Small Steps Will Take You to Big Goals," July 30, 2011, online post for her regular "Off the Couch" column, *Psychology Today*. Accessed at the following link:

https://www.psychologytoday.com/blog/the-couch/201107/small-steps-will-take-you-big-goals

See also, *Daydreaming: Unlock the Creative Power of Your Mind* (New York: Viking Adult, 1997).

7   The speech has been published in book form: George Saunders, *Congratulations, By the Way: Some Thoughts on Kindness* (New York: Random House, 2014). Quotations used above are taken from the commencement speech, available online at the following link: http://asnews.syr.edu/newsevents_2013/releases/george_saunders_convocation.html#sthash.HrGEeHxu.dpuf

Chapter 12: Adam

1   Gene Weingarten, "Pearls Before Breakfast: Can one of the nation's greatest musicians cut through the fog of a D.C. rush hour? Let's find out." *The [Washington] Post Magazine*, April 8, 2007. Italics mine.

2   James Weldon Johnson, *God's Trombones: Seven Negro Sermons in Verse* (New York: The Viking Press, 1927), 17.

3   Dorothy Gurney's poem "God's Garden" is widely reprinted—and widely displayed in gardens! A web version that relates to God's presence in difficult days is: http://www.anglicanjournal.com/articles/-nearer-god-s-heart-in-a-garden

4   Peter James Flamming, *God and Creation* (Nashville, TN: Broadman Press, 1985), 79.

Conclusion

1   Michael Yaconelli, *Messy Spirituality* (Grand Rapids, MI: Zondervan, 2007).

2   Sue Monk Kidd, *When the Heart Waits: Spiritual Direction for Life's Sacred Questions* (San Francisco, CA: Harper and Row, 1990), 152.

3   Some scholars make a great deal of difference between the two words used for *love* in John 20 and 21. In the Greek, one of those words is *agapol* and the other one is *filio*. My advice? Don't worry about that. They are different words, to be sure, but some experts exalt one above the other, and that is risky business. In fact, in John 20 and 21, the words were used interchangeably.

4   Don Wyrtzen, "Finally Home," Copyright 1971 Newspring, a Division of Brentwood-Benson Publishing (ASCAP).

Printed in the United States
By Bookmasters